T0208795

THEY'LL NEVER KNOW

SUMMARY OF SOME OF THE BEST AND WORST
KNOWN INSURANCE STORIES ACROSS THE DECADES.

Lori Power

ARCHWAY
PUBLISHING

Archway Publishing books may be ordered through booksellers or by contacting:

Archway Publishing
1663 Liberty Drive
Bloomington, IN 47403
www.archwaypublishing.com
844-669-3957

ISBN: 978-1-6657-3268-0 (sc)
ISBN: 978-1-6657-3267-3 (e)

Print information available on the last page.

Archway Publishing rev. date: 11/4/2022

CONTENTS

DISCLAIMER

The following is a compilation of insurance stories sourced from an abundance of information found via the World Wide Web, books, magazines, news articles, blogs, podcasts, among other sources, people, and presentations available to the author. They were summarized then organized according to topic title for ease of depiction.

In no particular order, the following information is for general reference and entertainment only. It is not intended as legal, tax, or insurance advice—certainly not financial planning. Changes to interpretations, conventions, legislation, or individual company policies may affect information. Please check with your insurance provider, lawyer, accounting, or human resources professional for further information.

This is not a peer-reviewed journal, a sponsored publication, or the product of editing. While the ideas and thoughts are often vital, pertinent, and relevant, the summaries, views, opinions, and experiences represented are just that—*view, opinions, and experiences*— and they belong solely to the author and do not represent those of people, the subjects, or anyone listed in the examples presented, institutions, or organizations that the author may or may not be associated with in a professional or personal capacity, unless explicitly stated. The views and opinions are not intended to malign any religion, ethnic group, club, organization, company, or individual.

The author makes no representations as to the accuracy or completeness of any information outlined. The author will not be liable for any errors or omissions in this information or for the availability of this content. The author will not be liable for any losses, injuries, or damages from the display or use of this information.

This content is dynamic and subject to changes from insurers, regulators, provincial governments, countries, legal precedents, and laws for which the summaries originate. The content expressed today may, in fact, change over time, legal penalties overturned, including the author's views, opinions, and experiences.

The author is not responsible or liable for anything anyone says in comments. Because publishing content is global, note that this book was developed in Canada through Canadian sources, unless referenced otherwise.

This book is for reference purposes only and by no means represents a legal document or counsel and should not be seen as such. Always consult legal and accounting advice.

INTRODUCTION

Why did I name the book *They'll Never Know*? Because ... frankly, I grew up with people saying that very line whenever they were "up to something." This adage was quickly followed by "How will *they* know?" and "Why would *they* care?"

First off, who are the "they" we're referencing? The authorities? The government? Any official? All the above? Certainly, someone with the money who the poets of these statements suddenly felt entitled to take from the source for whatever reason. All this line conveyed to me was people can convince themselves of anything when money is the motivator. Furthermore, as these summaries illustrate, just how far people will go once they have given themselves *permission to cross those lines*.

For as long as I have been in the insurance industry, I have been fascinated not only by insurance products themselves and their ability to help people, but also by people's attitude toward insurance. The simplicity of insurance is a beautiful thing. It is designed to cover off specific future risk elements—loss of life, loss of income, loss brought about by a catastrophic event—yet I've seen it complicated and butchered. But at the end of the day, it is meant to be simplistic and uncomplicated. Someone purchases a life insurance policy specifically for a beneficiary for a set dollar amount, and they pay a premium until their demise results in the payment of this policy to the person they chose as their recipient.

Simple. Done.

Over the years, I have seen abuse and gratitude working in kind, but somehow mixed in there is the entitlement attitude that there shouldn't be a cost for coverage. And even if there is a cost, then they're going to take more than what was paid. These are their stories.

Special shout out to Phoebe Judge, host and cocreator of "This Is Criminal" podcast (https://thisiscriminal.com) for germinating this idea.

Enjoy.

I will never apologize for committing insurance fraud. Insurance is for LOSERS who have no focus or control over their lives.

If you focus your mind, it's very easy to predict the future. This is why I've never made a single mistake in my whole life.

When you're like me, many "services" are obsolete. (I am also able to fly without planes, but that is neither here nor there.)

Frankly, I feel sorry for you people buying into the insurance scam.

Start predicting the future.

~Unknown[1]

---

[1] Source Unknown

CONSPIRACY

Fact or Fiction

CHAPTER 1

A Titanic Conspiracy—Could This Have Been the Largest Insurance Fraud in History?

Since the time of its sinking in 1912, the *Titanic* has had more than five hundred books written about it, never mind those that utilize the *voyage* as a backdrop for their fictional stories. Then there are the movies, from just days after the sinking through to famous James Cameron release in 1997, and six beyond that, and the twenty-two documentaries.

It would be safe then to say there is an absolute fascination with the ship—the sinking, the history, and the impact it has had on people around the world. As we chip away the ice of the multitude of conspiracy theories, at the heart of these conspiracies is the money. The ship was insured. There was a loss, and someone got paid. Is it the *who* that someone was that creates the great mystery? Is it the actual loss, or is it that someone benefitted from the loss?

Let's have a closer look.

Perhaps it surrounds people's fascination with the wealthy and their opulent lifestyles that started the conspiracy. Still a recognized name today in financial circles, John Pierpont Morgan, often referred to as simply J. P. Morgan, or today JPM, stands at the heart of most of the theories. This is mainly because the International Mercantile Marine Group was controlled by this American financier, who, at the time, dominated corporate finance on Wall Street. This was a man who had his hand in everything, from steel to electricity, the railroad, and many things in between. His massive influence was felt in finance, policy, and politics.

J. P. Morgan purchased White Star Line in 1902, which, among other ships, ultimately built luxury liner *Titanic*. Here was the opportunity to capitalize on the growing trend of oceanic travel. In 1908, White Star Line embarked on the building of three Olympic-class superliners to rival any hotel and instill opulence and glamour into every class of travel.

Advertised as the largest steamers in the world, the *Titanic*, the middle of this trilogy of ships, was heralded as the "Queen of the Ocean" and "Unsinkable." Therefore, if you must travel across the Atlantic, why not do it in style?

And here is where the conspiracy takes root. If this lavish ship was all this and so much more, why then did JPM pass on the maiden voyage?

The three luxury liners—the *Olympic*, *Titanic*, and *Britannic*—were constructed in the city of Belfast by the shipbuilding firm Harland and Wolff. The first of the trio to be completed was the RMS *Olympic*, launched on its maiden voyage in June 1911. Envisioned as the identical twin, the *Titanic* was already under construction when the Olympic set sail.

Could the launch of the *Olympic* have been rushed? Perhaps. Because during this initial trip, the *Olympic* was involved in an accident that damaged the ship to the stern, although this wasn't the end of her folly. Later that same year, September 20, in the Brambles Channel, Southampton, England, she collided with HMS

Hawke. As a result of this incident, both ships sustained considerable damage.

As mentioned before, the ships were insured, and White Star filed a claim with their insurer, Lloyd's of London. However, court proceedings determined White Star at fault, and the insurer declined the claim.

With considerable injury above and below the waterline, one third of the starboard side needed to be replaced with new steel and a propeller. With no insurance proceeds to cover the additional costs and no profits made from the *Olympic,* the parts were sourced from the *Titanic.* Since *Titanic* remained under construction, it was important that the *Olympic* be repaired to get back in open water and earning money.

When the *Olympic* went back to work, despite the repair, it did so with a permanent list to port.

To make matters worse, in February 1912, the *Olympic* suffered her third major incident when she ran atop a sunken ship and threw the propeller blade. White Star's flagship ocean liner had to return to Belfast for more costly reports just weeks before the launch of *Titanic.*

Because the *Olympic* and *Titanic* were virtually identical, to stem the financial bleeding, the conspiracy theory suggests the *Olympic* was repaired with supplies and fittings intended for *Titanic.* It's thought that this might have happened because White Star was losing money much faster than they could recuperate it, and this was an easy way to save funds. A whole marketing campaign was even imagined to recover the massive financial loss of the *Olympic* to date. In this, it is also suggested that *Olympic* underwent minor labelling adjustments to reintroduce her as the "Unsinkable *Titanic*" on April 10.

According to the conspiracy theories, the plan itself was a simple one. If the *Olympic* could not be profitable because of the already-substantial damage, then she'd be sunk to recover costs through the insurance proceeds. This would leave White Star to get back to business with the remaining two superliners. The fresh start would see the RMS *Titanic* take on the identity of the fallen *Olympic*, and they could begin the build on the third.

The acceptable truth is the ship struck the iceberg late in the evening on April 14, 1912, off the coast of Newfoundland. There, the superliner sunk into the icy North Atlantic waters at 2:20 a.m. of April 15, taking 1,517 souls with her.

Plot variation of the events suggested that the forty-six-thousand-ton ocean liner was struck by a German U-boat. However, because of the obvious timeline—the ship sunk two years prior to the start of World War 1—it's hard to see the plausibility in that theory.

Another alternative notion is that the *Olympic*, disguised as the *Titanic*, unintentionally ran over their supposed rescue ship, whose lights were out in their covert waiting at that location to pull survivors from the sinking craft. The strategic placement of this rescue ship would just happen to be in the proximity to pick up the mayday. This distress call, of course, would only happen after the *unsinkable* ship drove directly into the iceberg it was never intending to miss.

Here is where this intrigue gets interesting. Under the command of Edward Smith, the fateful night was apparently clear and starry. Edward Smith was running the ship at speed. Sailors, who were well experienced at crossing the Atlantic, would know the area to be quite littered with these floating mountains. Watchmen were on also duty, specifically to hail any obstructions or danger. This is why it is suggested that the plotters would have planned their timing and location well in advance, never intending on any loss of life in the process.

In these conditions, some have even suggested that the iceberg would have been visible much sooner than reported. Apparently, officers later testified that icebergs could be spotted six to eight miles from the deck and even further from the crow's nest. With a rounding pace of 1,800 feet, one conspiracy suggested the ship would have ample space to avoid the collision. Yet the attempted turn was not made until the obstruction was but four hundred yards away. At this point, the reversal of the engines and turning to port placed the ship in a position of maximum damage.

By any measure, according to the survivor reports, action was not swift by the crew to fire flares or prepare the limited lifeboats to get the 2,224 passengers and staff members to safety. In fact, it was supposedly forty-five minutes after the collision before the pumps were turned on, the flooded areas locked down, and a further hour after that before the lifeboats were fully deployed.

After the distress calls and flares, several ships responded they were on their way. Certainly, the SS *Californian*, part of the International Mercantile Marine Group fleet, was a mere nineteen miles away but seemed to take no action despite telegraphing several times with its exact location. Twelve miles off its original course, the *Californian* had no passengers aboard and a cargo of wool sweaters, yet it failed to appear.

Instead, RMS *Carpathia* finally arrived two hours after the superliner took her last breath to collect the survivors in the icy black water.

Added to the mystique is the fact that several high-profile people, including J. P. Morgan, cancelled their reservation just hours before departure. Still, millionaires like the prominent builder of hotels and skyscrapers—Col. Jacob Astor, banker and owner of Macy's Isidor Straus, and American businessman of mining machinery Benjamin Guggenheim—all went down with the ship.

If this had been a calculated insurance fraud with a controlled rescue, it seemed ill-fated caused by poor planning.

Lloyd's of London paid the £1 million claim within thirty days of the fateful sinking. That's not even including the insurance that would have been payable on insured lives, lost items, costly art, and jewelry.

After the loss, the *Olympic*, with its three significant accidents behind her, went on to serve an additional twenty-five years on the ocean and encountered more significant crashes in 1918 and 1934.

Meanwhile, after her completion, the transatlantic ocean liner, HMHS *Britannic*, was recommissioned as a hospital ship and served between the United Kingdom and Dardanelles. On November 21, 1916, an explosion from a naval mine of the Imperial German Navy sank her in fifty-five minutes, killing thirty people.

HISTORICAL

Where It All Began

CHAPTER 2

Time Immoral

I t may be safe to say that so long as there have been assets, a currency, or better put, a value perceived, there has been insurance to protect those assets; insurance being conceived to protect against a risk of loss, especially in commerce, which has been going on since … well, the beginning or at least the dawn of trade.

Archeologist have found evidence outlining the laws of trading dating all the way back to the first Babylonian Empire. This includes outlines of early insurance, the necessity of using a shipping agent, factor, or ship charterer in the event of total loss.

Equally true then would be, with these financial instruments in place and some entity willing to protect that bargain in the form of we would term now to be insurance, there would, therefore, be fraud; someone wanting to double dip, someone seeing an opportunity to collect on an opportunity.

Some of the earliest proof of such dealings in insurance can be seen from the writings of satirist Marcus Valerius Martialis. Known as Martial, he is famous for his twelve books of epigrams published between AD 86 and 103, where he writes in great detail about the human foibles of the time. In these short often-witty poems, Martial would recount city life, scandals, and romances. Within the 1,561 epigrams, there is clear evidence as well of the growth of insurance fraud within the Roman Empire.

> *Tongilianus, you paid two hundred for your house.*
> *An accident too common in this city destroyed it. You*
> *collected ten times more. Doesn't it seem, I pray, That*
> *you set fire to your own house, Tongilianus?*

Book III, No 52[2]

    Later evidence in 300 BC gives rise to typical insurance fraud not so unlike what may be found in the modern era. Here, a Greek merchant named Hegestratos took out a large insurance policy known at the time as bottomry on his corn trade along the Mediterranean. It is important to note that engaging with a third-party to protect the value of goods being traded outside one's own village was commonplace by this era.

    The term "bottomry" referred to the bottom of a ship or the keel and was used as an exchange tool against loss whereby the ship itself would be the collateral. The merchant would borrow the money against the value of the ship and agree to pay it back with interest. If the trader reneged on the loan, then the lender would claim the cargo and the boat used.

    Someone willing to pay for a loss that this early Greek entrepreneur felt couldn't be proved offered nothing but opportunity. Here was the chance to sell his cargo, sink the ship, and claim the total loss. Hegestratos was even going to make the creditors pay him to rebuild, and he'd be much better off with the money from the sale and a new ship thrown in. Sound thinking, some may say, for how hard could it be to dupe the lenders?

---

[2] https://www.tertullian.org/fathers/martial_epigrams_book03.htm

Hegestratos kept his part simple. As the story goes, Hegestratos planned to offload his cargo, sink his empty boat, keep the loan, and sell the corn. If he had been successful, of course, the story of Hegestratos wouldn't have made it into this book.

As recorded, the scheme failed. Poor Hegestratos apparently drowned trying to escape his crew and passengers when they caught him in the act. Seems even back then people didn't appreciate having to pay more for someone else's greed.

ON THE MORE NEFARIOUS SIDE ...

Where Vantage Point Skews Perception

CHAPTER 3

The Disgusting History of "Insurance" Underwriting Slavery

As we'll come to see, insurance, by and large, is a financial instrument, and like any tool, it can be wielded for positive and negative intentions. While a hammer has many uses, one of which may be for building a house, it can also be used as weapon. So too is the case here for insurance.

There was no shortage of personal trepidation in including this aspect of insurance in history as part of the manuscript because this is not a political document, nor should it be seen as such. This is included for information in the light of "we should know" this is part of our insurance past.

To summarize the atrocious history of insurance in the slave trade, we must start at the beginning. As noted, insurance and trade go hand in hand. When human beings became cargo for trade, there entered insurance for the protection of that transaction.

While it may be hard to believe in this modern light, documents suggest insuring slaves at sea dates back to the fifteenth century in the Mediterranean. It is true: This is not a research document, and in all likelihood, slavery predates this as well, but actual documentation where insurance was used specifically to cover the loss of humans is illustrated from this period.

Equally true, from the beginning of insuring people as cargo, there has been the moral debate of human versus property. Depending on the era, individual people as cargo impacted the contracts being sold. In these early policies, humans were covered under what was termed "maritime cargo."

Slavery and civilization have coexisted for centuries. Records show the bargaining of people has been documented in ancient Egypt, China, India, Persia, Greece, and the Roman Empire to name a few. Outside other nations that practice slavery between the sixteenth and nineteenth centuries, more than 12.5 million Africans were forcibly transported. As a leading slave nation, between 1761 and 1807, its abolition, Britain had transported about 40 percent of enslaved Africans and insured this through companies, such as the London Assurance Corporation, as "risk" termed as cargo against "perils of the sea."

These risks included but weren't limited to the usual risk of transoceanic commerce but also high crew and slave morbidity. Claims were payable for slave revolt or resistance, exchange value uncertainties, and the default of payments for the purchase of the new slaves after the delivery.

Not limited to the British, many early American insurance companies, such as Baltimore Life Insurance Company of Maryland, North Carolina Mutual, Mutual Benefit Life and Fire of Louisiana, and Greensboro Mutual Life targeted domestic slave traders to grow their business. By 1860, advertisements were placed in newspapers, auction houses, hirers' offices, tobacco factories, tobacco exchange, and principal depots in urban centers to promote sales.

By issuing policies that reflected the dual designation of slaves as people and property, it is suggested the insurers had concerns about how to underwrite the risk. In commerce, to assign a risk, the institution would have to be able to use historical data to understand mortality by age, occupation, or location. These organizations had no such actuarial documentation to rely upon.

Added to this lack of information was the moral hazard created by market value decline. How could the insurer assign future value to a human being? Impacted by political and economic climates, the value of an individual may deteriorate more rapidly than anticipated. Would the market for trading in people continue and for how long?

The risk of someone being seen more valuable dead than alive meant the purchase of several policies would need to be limited. Companies grappled with rendering the slave more valuable dead than alive.

These unanswerable financial criteria typical in the underwriting of insurance lead insurers to deem that slaves could only be insured by one policy in the stipulated employment role up to two-thirds of their value. Added to this, they would only provide coverage for, in most cases, up to a maximum of seven years. Because of growing underwriting concerns, companies typically doubled the premium for black lives and would regularly review the policies for changes in health or occupation. In fact, policies were voided in cases where the employment was changed without written consent of the insurer or if it were found that the slave owner purchased multiple policies.

Many of the polies purchased were confined to enslaved people involved in what was considered valuable work, like blacksmithing, lumber, carpentry, factory, mining, railroad, and steamboats. Not a lot is known of plantation owners purchasing policies on their slave labor, and it is suspected that they were treated more in line with livestock. It is doubtful plantation owners even bothered to purchase coverage on their enslaved people.

Northern insurance companies, like Nautilus Mutual Life Insurance Company, which became New York Life Insurance, Aetna, and AIG, began to sell policies in the 1840s in what was proving to be a lucrative market to the South, where they ran ads to encourage slave owners to protect their most valuable commodity.

As with so many financial instruments, what could be wielded one way could also be manipulated another way. Not to be overlooked, insurance also became valuable in the emancipation of individual slaves. As is seen today, where people may use their policies in the purchase of home or on a loan, at the time, as a means of raising capital, people of both races, free blacks, and former slaves would purchase policies on people they intended to free. In these cases, the insurance served as collateral until the slave was able to earn their own purchase price.

CHAPTER 4

Genocide and Life Insurance, World War II

I nsurance is purchased as a risk mitigator. What happens then when a government declares arbitrarily that all policies are nil and void or are payable to an entity not party to the contract?

This is exactly what happened to the Jewish population in Germany in the 1930s. Consider for a moment the sheer volume of commercial insurance coverage for the many German Jewish business owners in that decade. Then try to fathom the loss of their businesses, the destruction or confiscation of their property by the state. And on top of that, adding insult to injury, the German government of the day determined there would be no payout of coverage from their insurance policies despite premiums paid and up to date. In fact, they were no longer entitled to file a claim.

This leads us to another equally dark period in insurance history.

Insurance products did and still do offer the protection of one's life and property and was, by and large, a staple in most European communities. With growing political unrest, sales for insurance products boomed, and many insurers grew rich in the process. Then when the atrocities ended and the survivors started to pick up the pieces with next to nothing and no one to go home to, no finances to speak of, no hard assets, they sought to claim on the life insurance of lost relatives only to be declined.

Tens of thousands of Holocaust survivors tried to claim on policies for those lost to the concentration camps. With slips of paper salvaged often from wreckage or somehow maintained during their time in the camps with the only item of value they had left, policy numbers and names of the insured, insurance companies refused to pay. Instead, insurer after insurer demand actual signed copies of the policies and death certificates.

Even though it is well known that the governing Germans at the time didn't issue death certificates to those they murdered, the insurance companies still refused to pay.

Despite overwhelming evidence that more than eight hundred thousand policies existed, the insurers refuse to release any list of names of covered people. Instead, they cited their privacy policy in which a privacy policy likely didn't exist when the insurance contracts were originally purchased. Lawsuits from survivors against more than twenty European insurance companies first began in the 1990s; however, most of the suits were eventually dropped or settled. Estimates suggest that the value of the insurance would amount to around $18 billion.

Founded in 1998, the International Commission on Holocaust-Era Insurance Claims (ICHEIC) was committed to settling the issue of outstanding life insurance policies during the Nazi era.

Of the more than seventy thousand claims that have been filed, it is estimated that only 9,600 have reached a final ruling with less than five hundred cases settling for approximately $12,000 per claimant. It seems to some that instead of working on behalf of the relatives of these unjustly prosecuted people, the bureaucratic whirly wheel spins nonstop requiring that

- A claim needs to be filed with the ICHEIC office
- The claim is checked against a central registry
- If the name (or a variation) appears in the central registry, a search for the actual policy is conducted in the archives
- Restitution offices are contacted to determine if previous compensation has been provided
- An offer is made if
  - The policyholder was persecuted under the Nazi regime
  - No record of compensation is found, but the person's name is in the register, and a contract has been signed
  - The policy was confiscated or paid into a blocked account and not paid to the state

(source: *Allianz During The Nazi Era*[3])

Corporate indifference is what may best describe the insurers by the remaining beneficiaries. Many imply much was done to disqualify rather than remedy deserving relations. Insurers trying to justify why they cannot pay the policies suggest many policies had been cancelled between 1933 and 1938, when the Nazi government stepped up its anti-Semitic actions. Some survivors were even told the contracts were terminated in the 1940s. For the survivors to scoff at such a notion would be an understatement since this would have been when they and their deceased relatives were, in fact, inmates of the state in the concentration camps.

If these excuses weren't enough, to further complicate the payout, underwriters insinuate that at the time these contracts had to be paid into a blocked account used by the state to collect tax, debts, and special fees imposed on the Jewish people or were confiscated directly by the Reich.

Imagine, as a beneficiary, trying to make an insurance claim and being told, so sorry, your claim was paid out to the Nazi party.

---

[3] https://www.allianz.com/content/dam/onemarketing/azcom/Allianz_com/about-us/who-we-are/documents/Allianz_during_the_Nazi_era.pdf

To further add insult to injury, let's not forget the property insurance that these same insurers placed on the death camps themselves. The SS apparently purchased the insurance to preserve the fiction of legitimate business to cover the slave labor of the camps.

The overreaching issue here was never about the value of the insurance payout but the ethical duty of the insurers to do the right thing.

ACROSS MULTIPLE LINES

The Largest Claim in History

CHAPTER 5

9/11 Insured Payouts

I t's amazing how much the world changed in one hundred minutes on Tuesday, September 11, 2001. The ripple effects of that attack are still felt globally, whether by the change in business, the way we conduct ourselves, security, and the way we view insurance and insurable circumstances.

The shock and loss caused by 9/11 were extreme and unforeseen. As is common in the aftermath of disasters, when the dust settles and people gather to attempt their rebuild, they seek financial restitution. For those with insured coverage, they look to their policies for the protection it provides financially.

To be clear, insured loss is not the same as economic loss and certainly nothing to the emotional loss of the estimated three thousand and more lives and close to that number in injuries. Here, we will focus on the lesser of these, the insured loss, which is cited to be the largest insurance loss of any natural or man-made disaster in history.

As a result of the terrorist attacks, many lines of insurance, including but certainly not limited to life, property, liability, business interruption, commercial loss, aviation, workers' compensation, disability, and benefits were all impacted in some way. It's not hard to realize why 9/11 had such a wide-ranging impact when you consider that two of the tallest buildings in the world on some of the richest real estate soil were decimated by aircrafts flying directly into them. Not to mention the fallout and destruction on the surrounding office space and complete business closure or shut down, which undulated out like the initial shock wave. The ramifications would last years and, some may argue, decades.

Actuaries and underwriters use tables and formulas used to predict expected payouts over time, time being the critical element in the equation. An expected payout all at once, over multiple lines of insurance, did not, up to that moment, factor into any previously considered calculation.

While one may expect that insurance would have been the last item on anyone's list that day, that was, in fact, not the case. Certainly, within minutes of the accounts being broadcast, insurers were fielding calls on estimated costs, questions around if they were prepared to pay and even if they could pay. Additional elements on whether the loss may feature into any existing exclusion clause under the policy for act of war or terrorism were very real contractual elements, which needed to be dealt with in a reasonable manner whether this kind of event would be added as a future exclusion. Further queries wondered if there would be cost-sharing with the government. This topic alone became a public policy debate, which would take years to settle, if one can consider the debate settled.

Some estimates suggest a staggering loss of more than US$39.4 billion broken down by approximately 15,200 commercial claims, 31,500 in personal property, and 4,300 for auto claims. As time goes on, those numbers will change. World Trade Center Properties and others associated with the developer collected about $4.1 billion in insurance, though they claimed to be entitled to $14 billion. This stands outside the enormity of claimants for life, injury, and disability.

WHERE THE MONEY GOES?

Who's Benefiting?

CHAPTER 6

When Insurance Money Is Used to Fund Terrorism

While we explored how insurance has been used as a financial tool for good and ill in the purchasing of policies, let's explore situations of payout. What happens when the beneficiary money is received as a result of a crime and used in criminal enterprise?

We've seen the devastation resulting from outside terror attacks; here's an example of the homegrown kind.

Some may say, even as a young boy, rebel and insurgent behavior of guerrilla fighters absorbed Isaac Aguigui's imagination and future ambition. Though he would grow to be an enlisted soldier, having early exposure to government as a messenger, he seems to have never lost that initial fascination of taking over from within.

Prior to being convicted in 2014 of murdering his pregnant wife for the insurance money, Isaac founded the homegrown terrorist outfit Forever Enduring Always Ready[4] (FEAR). This was when Isaac was a twenty-two-year-old army private married to army ser-

---

[4] https://www.swordandscale.com/forever-enduring-always-ready/

geant Deirdre Aguigui, who had recently returned from an overseas posting. In reality, part of the motivation for the murder of his wife was specifically to funnel the funds received in her insurance payout to bankroll this terror business.

Though Deirdre's death in July 2011 was considered highly suspicious, no charges were initially laid. Evidence at the time proved scant of what specifically killed her. The military's autopsy found more than twenty bruises and scrapes on her body, including on her head and back, but nothing appeared fatal. Wounds on wrists appeared to match a pair of handcuffs found on the couple's bed. Because it had been known they utilized these kinds of instruments in their sexual play, the official cause of death was not determined.

Isaac seemed little perturbed by the proceedings of his spouse's death. Quickly moving on, he utilized his relationships from within the US military. Working systematically, Isaac set about targeting disgruntled army cohorts to build his own militia. Once formed, they created targets from within the country. This included laying plans to bomb a public park, poisoning apple crops, and infiltrating the drug trade to name a few.

Although Isaac had been a page at the republican convention when then Pres. Barack Obama was running for office, the suggestions are that Isaac disapproved of the socialist politics being presented. This then sparks the seeds of dissent where he planned to seize control of the United States and eventually assassinate the president.

Initially cleared of suspicion, directly after Deirdre's death, Isaac claimed the US$400,000 life insurance policy and the US$100,000 provided by the American military for funeral costs. He proceeded to use a large chunk of this money to purchase arsenal—guns and bomb components. They were stored for when they would be needed.

During this time, Isaac went on to murder two more people who apparently got in the way of his plans. It was only after Isaac was found guilty of murdering Tiffany York and fellow army buddy

Michael Roark, whom Isaac suspected may leak his plans as they were in the process of stockpiling weapons and ammunition, that the case involving his wife was re-established.

Further investigation and evidence based on his own boasting outlined how the death was said to have occurred. Apparently, he coaxed his wife to wear handcuffs during sex and then suffocating her with a plastic bag over her head. The medical examiner said she was strangled while struggling violently against handcuffs behind her back.

Prosecutors implied that because Isaac had been trained how to kill without leaving identifiable marks, he used this tactic on his wife when he needed her out of the picture.

Isaac is serving a life sentence of life without parole at a Georgia prison.

CHAPTER 7

Why Are Pirates Called "Pirates"? Because They Arrrrrrre!

This is no swashbuckling tale of high seas and romance. Instead, modern-day piracy is as deadly as it ever was with the stakes increasing steadily every year. From modern-day slavery to poaching and theft, hijacking, and kidnapping, piracy is a real and ongoing global problem. The world over law enforcement docs what they can to stay ahead of or shut these operations down. Yet despite best efforts, the numbers and participants continue to plague legitimate businesspeople, sea routes, and their customers.

Of course, pirates are funded by the illegal dollar, but more disturbing is the fact that despite their nefarious intentions, these vessels are most often covered by marine insurance in the event of loss or damage. This means that regardless of the actions that caused the peril when these vessels are sunk or impaired, the ships are quickly replaced, and the criminals are back out on open water to wreak their havoc with to no overall loss of funding to slow them down.

Take the fishing industry as an example. There are fleets of what are referred to as "illegal, unreported, and unregulated[5]" (IUU) boats that reportedly not only do untold damage to the worldwide fishing operations, but also cost billions annually from legitimate business ventures. Yet just like legal vessels, they are often covered by third-party liability insurance with little to no change or limitations on coverage despite their unlawful trade and greater "risk." It is suggested that when reviewing the return on investment, because of the nature of their industry, the larger payout for their activities brought about by expected damage far outweighs the actual increased cost of the premiums.

Although marine insurance is mandatory on vessels of a certain size, refusing coverage for IUU ships would remove the economic safety net these criminal organizations rely upon to keep them active. However, expecting insurance companies to have that kind of upfront knowledge is unreasonable. While some studies further suggest that, at a minimum, insurance carriers should limit or modify coverage in these situations, the underwriters seem at a loss as to how to implement or even where to begin to gain a purchase hold on this problem.

This continues to be an ongoing debate.

---

[5] https://www.fao.org/iuu-fishing/en/

AND WHEN YOU'RE CAUGHT IN THE MIDDLE,

Is There Insurance for That?

CHAPTER 8

Guaranteed Ransom or No Concessions

Those impacted by acts of terror, piracy, random violence outside their control, and those who must work in war-torn areas is a whole other area of insurable coverage. Taking reasonable precautions, the question still arises: What happens if you are abducted or become victim of pirates or another criminal element through no fault of your own?

This is where kidnapping insurance comes into play.

Randomly, we hear about people being abducted, kidnapped, watch movies about the same, but the behind-the-scenes work of getting that person back seems a little vague. In fact, there seems very little publicity about this insurance—a distinct lack of marketing.

Who sells it or even where to buy it seems like it may need a secret handshake and an alleyway deal to find out. Of course, this is not the case, but the mystic surrounds of the coverage is very real and on purpose.

The anonymity is intentional. This is because a significant part of what makes the insurance work when it needs to work in the deadliest situations is the policy provision of privacy. The truth is the general public isn't supposed to know. No one is to be privy to who has this insurance, when they have it, or how much they are covered for in the event of need.

In fact, with ransom demands in the millions of dollars, the policy must be kept secret. If publicly known in advance of a kidnapping, the policy would be voided. With the details kept in confidence, those associated confirm kidnapping is not a shrinking market for criminals. While very few cases of kidnapping make media headlines, this isn't because the cases are few and far between. Quite the opposite. Because of the clandestine nature of the contract, those in field operations do much to keep headlines to a minimum or nonexistent.

For the general public who may believe this level of extra insurance may fit the expectations for what the wealthy or celebrity may require, this would be a false assumption. Another mis-conjecture would be to believe incidents only occur in certain countries or by pirates in African waters, kidnappers in the Middle East, or guerrillas in the South American jungle.

Actual statistics are staggering. In Mexico, for instance, a favorite tourist destination, the average kidnapper's earnings are reported at more than $50 million annually. According to some reports in this area of expertise, Latin America remains the most dangerous region for kidnapping threats, while Nigeria and Venezuela are growing in revenue-generation through this kind of criminal activity.

Initially created back in the 1930s, the purpose of this kind of speciality insurance is to cover the costs of ransom, extortion, or hijacking demands for the safety and safe return of the covered insured person. Most contracts will include evacuation provisions from remote or dangerous areas around the globe. Additionally, and some may say most importantly, the policies cover the cost of the highly trained experts brought in to confirm proof of life and negotiate the terms of release.

Statistics show that 61 percent of all kidnapping worldwide are employees and/or dependents of corporations, not the owner. This is why enterprises, organizations, missionary groups, and humanitarian expeditions, to name a few examples, will purchase this coverage for the safety of their people traveling to remote areas known for violence.

Something that may not be well known is that the insurance policy for this purpose cannot be purchased for more than the insured is actually worth. Further, the policy will only pay out—be able to be claimed against—once the ransom is paid. The money is never released upfront. Once the negotiator is assigned, the insured's family or estate is tasked with raising the money by whatever means are available—liquidating assets—and then and only once the deal has been finalized will the insurance claim be processed. This is done for several reasons, including but not limited to keeping the criminal element out and to avoid fraud. Again, if it is known ahead of time by anyone other than the parties to the insurance that the insured is covered for this speciality risk, the policy is void.

The difference for those traveling without this insurance when they are operating in "known" hotspots can mean months or even years spent as a hostage and perhaps even death when the kidnappers have nothing to gain from keeping the victim alive.

Alberta, Canada resident Amanda Lindhout recounts her fifteen-month ordeal in the book *A House in the Sky*[6] when she and another man were taken hostage in August 2008 near Mogadishu, Somalia. She lost hair, nails, teeth caused by malnourishment and torture. Amanda was twenty-seven at the time. She has said had she been covered through a kidnapping policy, she may have been freed within days or weeks. Instead, her family incurred massive debt to raise the $600,000 ransom demand, and release only happened once they hired a negotiator.

[6] https://www.amazon.ca/House-Sky-Memoir-Amanda-Lindhout/dp/1451651481/ref=sr_1_1?dchild=1&keywords=Amanda+Lindhout&qid=1622832322&sr=8-1

DEATH AS A RESULT OF CRIMINAL ACTIVITY

Is Insurance Payable?

CHAPTER 9

When Life's the Bomb …

Sometimes even the best-laid plans backfire. A recoil, when you're working with explosives, can prove deadly, especially when you're doing so as a result of criminal intent.

On October 11, 1990, Roger Arbic of Montreal, Quebec, purchased a life insurance policy from Transamerica Life Insurance Company of Canada.[7] He named his spouse, Danielle Goulet, as his sole beneficiary. Then on January 22, 1994, fifty-one-year-old Arbic, a known gangster, died when the bomb he was planting in a vehicle at Dorval Airport blew up and, contrary to his intention, resulted in his death.

As named beneficiary, Danielle, not representing the estate or heir, personally claimed the $50,000 life policy due in accordance with the policy. Even though there was no clause included in the policy, which precluded criminal activity, at the time, Transamerica Life declined the claim. They stated that because Roger died as a result of committing a crime, no amount should be payable.

---

[7] https://decisions.scc-csc.ca/scc-csc/news/fr/item/1146/index.do

The "should be" doesn't really align with contracts. Contracts, by and large, are what is written is what is acted upon.

While it is true that Roger Arbic was a known criminal with a history of armed robberies, Transamerica Life did issue a life insurance policy without ever citing this would bar a beneficiary's eligibility to make a claim. They neither checked nor confirmed at the time that his criminal nature would come to cause any issue at the time of claim.

True, when purchased, the policy included a two-year suicide clause. However, at the time of his death, four years later, that clause was no longer valid, and the nature of his death wasn't debated as suicidal. Additionally, there was nothing stated in the contract of insurance precluding payment should the life insured die while committing a crime, therefore, Danielle's lawyers argued the full amount of the policy should be payable.

The insurer argued that public order justified refusal to pay when the death had occurred during the commission of a crime. They additionally noted that because of this criminal activity, Roger knowingly put himself in harm's way, which greatly increased the risks associated with the loss of life.

Again, this did not factor into the discussion at the time of purchase.

Danielle proved successful in winning the case in the Superior Court and the Court of Appeal. The decision found in favor of the beneficiary as "there was no evidence to show that the insured knew he was going to die when he planted the bomb," said Mr. Justice Louis LeBel. "Even though planting a bomb is an inherently dangerous activity, it is wrong to say that the death that resulted was not an accident."

In the end, what swayed the argument when the Supreme Court of Canada cited in its favor of the beneficiary was because as beneficiary, Danielle was innocent of the crime being committed and should not be adversely punished for her husband's wrongdoings.

They indicated that there was no link or proof of her involvement in his actions. Further, she would have no way of knowing his actions would result in his untimely death.

The contractual freedom Transamerica Life has meant they must establish the limits the risk covered and the conditions on which the indemnity is payable at the time of purchase of the policy. The acceptance of premium payment bound the contract. To try to establish or enforced changes once the policy claim was received and payment expected was not within boundaries of the contract.

At the time of his death, Roger's policy was in force, the premium was paid, and there was nothing to suppose that the policy would not be enforceable.

Even though the bomb he was planting was obviously criminal and it could be surmised he was involved in a criminal activity, there was no cause to support this would decline a claim. There was no proof of suicide, and even if it had been death by suicide, the clause for such had lapsed. The named beneficiary, his spouse, Danielle, was not linked to this criminal activity. Therefore, the courts concluded, the appeals were dismissed with costs, and the claim paid.

CHAPTER 10

The Drug Mule

In another landmark case also involving Transamerica Life Insurance Co. of Canada, the court ruled in favor of the beneficiary when the claimant, a drug mule, died in Bolivia when the container of cocaine he had swallowed leaked, resulting in his death.

In addition to the precedent setting 1990 Roger Arbic case, section 118 of the Ontario *Insurance Act* states that "a contravention of any criminal or other law in force in Ontario or elsewhere does not, by that fact alone, render unenforceable a claim for indemnity under a contract of insurance."

At the time of his death, Maria Oldfield and her husband Paul Oldfield were separated. In January 1995, in lieu of any spousal or child support, they agreed that her husband would maintain his $250,000 life insurance policy, leaving her sole beneficiary until their children reached the age of majority.

At the time of his death, Maria's husband was carrying thirty condoms filled with cocaine in his stomach. One of the condoms burst, causing him to go into cardiorespiratory arrest. Despite the criminal activity, as with Arbic, the death was considered unintentional and accidental. There was no speculation of suicide.

At the time of the claim, Transamerica Life[8] refused the Oldfield claim on the grounds of public policy rule that the courts will not recognize a benefit accruing to a criminal from his crime. Put another way, no one should benefit from an illegal activity.

Based on the signed policy contract, the court did not agree.

The policy stated, "[I]n the absence of fraud this policy will be incontestable after it has been in force during the Insured's lifetime for 2 years from the date of issue, or the date of reinstatement or change, whichever is latest, except for non-payment of premiums."

The insurance policy did not address whether proceeds were payable when the insured died as a result of his own criminal act.

Maria was not linked to the unlawful behavior. In fact, she had been listed as the beneficiary long before the criminal activity took place and, therefore, was not considered a party to the act. Because of this proven timeline, the court further concluded that she was not benefitting nor profiting from the illegal behavior.

Moreover, "To deny recovery would penalize the victim for the insured's antisocial behavior," Mr. Justice Jack Major wrote. "To permit recovery in such circumstances will not create a new cottage industry where insurance companies will vie to insure criminal activities."

Using this same logic as the insurer applied for denying the claim, the court held that Transamerica could not be allowed to abrogate its responsibilities and refuse to pay the claim. So while people cannot benefit from committing a crime nor can innocent third parties be penalized for the wrongdoing of others.

---

[8] https://decisions.scc-csc.ca/scc-csc/news/fr/item/1146/index.do?q=Paul+Oldfield+&submit=Recherche

CHAPTER 11

The Insanity Plea

n 1992, Ved and Kamlesh Dhingra[9] separated. Despite the estrangement, in 1998, Ved acquired group life insurance and named Kamlesh as his beneficiary. Under the same policy, Kamlesh was also named as an insured for life insurance worth approximately $50,000 and Ved the listed beneficiary. Then in 2006, Ved killed his former wife by hitting her several times with a marble statue and claimed the proceeds of the life insurance.

He won.

Ved had been suffering from serious mental illness for years prior to the murder of his former wife. In 2008, when Ved was charged with second-degree murder, the insurer paid the life proceeds to the court to discharge. However, as a result of Ved's known and continued mental illness, he was found not criminally responsible for the crime.

Kamlesh's son petitioned to have the proceeds of the life insurance paid into his mother's estate, of which he was the acting

[9] https://www.cbc.ca/news/canada/mentally-ill-man-crown-battle-for-slain-womans-insurance-payout-1.1272709

administrator, rather than to be paid to Ved. Ved, on the other hand, opposed this request and brought an application to have the money paid to him as he was the beneficiary.

This resulted in a back-and-forth in the courts. While it's true he was found not criminally responsible, that didn't change the fact that Kamlesh was dead because of her husband having killed her. So the question came down to intent and how this decision would impact the public policy rule of not having someone profit from their crime.

The argument ended in April 2012, when the court agreed, after appeal, that there was no rationale for applying the public policy rule when a person was found not criminally responsible. By definition, when a person is found not criminally responsible by mental disorder, they are not "morally responsible" for their actions, and therefore, the proceeds from the life insurance could not be withheld.

This case, in definition, rather than criminal action, is reminiscent of the 1962 decision of Kathleen Nordstrom. In this situation, Kathleen burned down their home while her husband John Nordstrom was inside, resulting to his death. Because she was the administratrix of the estate, she petitioned to have rights of the widow in a share of the estate.

As she had been found by the trial judge at the time to be insane based upon expert testimony and witnesses, they held that when she set the fire, she "did not appreciate the nature and quality of her act or know that it was wrong," and therefore, she was entitled to her portion of the estate as an inheritance befitting a widow.

FAKE AND BAKE

Watch Out for the Next Wave

CHAPTER 12

That "Sinking" Sensation

I t's October 2016, and the economy is not in great shape. Even the golden sands on the California southern coastline are losing their shimmer. The fish may be biting and the tackle cleaned and ready, but where are the customers? Sure, tourism was up 3 percent year over year in the state, but visitors didn't seem to be interested in booking charters for the sport of fishing or at least not with Mission Bay's Eclipse Sportfishing.

Eclipse's owners Christopher Switzer and Mark Gillette[10] see that their reservations are down, and they're having trouble to keep up with the rising costs of repairs and maintenance of the fifty-seven-foot Commander. So they decide there is another solution.

Of course, the captains have insurance on the vessel. Why not collect? That would solve their financial troubles, and they could start again. There's nothing like wiping the slate clean for a fresh start. Step 1 of this solution is to ditch the boat. Boats sink all the

---

[10] https://www.justice.gov/usao-sdca/pr/two-san-diego-ship-owners-plead-guilty-after-intentional-sinking-insurance-money

time. The process should be easy. All they need to do is ensure they have a means of getting back to shore safely so they can file the claim and collect.

All the best-laid plans washed away ...

Located close to San Diego, on October 11, Christopher and Mark took the boat out, supposedly on their way to Long Beach. But within seven miles of Dana Point, they called in the coast guard for support.

It was later learned that they paused the voyage midway to begin sabotaging the vessel. The first step of their plan included destroying the plastic PVC piping in the ship's engine room. This would render the boat helpless in the water. The destruction of the tubing allowed sea water to glut the craft. Trying to time the sinking and the escape proved cumbersome. With the commander not flooding fast enough, the two then proceeded to puncture the bulkhead and to pump in sea water in themselves for faster sinking. On a roll to be rid of the burden, they caused additional damage to the water-supply plumbing to bait tanks and the fish holds, moving the valves into the open position.

However, despite all that effort, the boat never did fully sink.

Expecting the boat to be submerged within an hour, the pair called in support from the coast guard and Orange County sheriff's deputies. They claimed a loss of power and unknown flooding. A helicopter and boats were launched as part of the rescue at sea mission. The men were saved from the partially submerged Commander and divers went into action. The professionals from the coast guard managed to refloat the Commander with airbags and then tow it back to San Diego.

The plan broken down further once the boat was safely back on shore. There, the salvage team quickly assessed the situation and reported the damage appeared intentional. Still, Christopher and Mark maintained the pretense. Only at the point when the insurance adjuster arrived did the two come clean. Instead of allowing the adjuster on board, Mark told the coast guard they wouldn't be filing for insurance.

The pair could have faced a penalty of ten years in prison and a $250,000 fine; they received probation. Christopher and Mark pleaded guilty in February 2017. During court proceedings, the two admitted to intentionally putting themselves and the first-responders at risk as well as filing false reports. They were sentenced to eighteen-month probation and required to pay more than $15,000 to cover the costs of the rescue.

It is unlikely they would suggest their financial situation improved as a result.

CHAPTER 13

No Body—No Dough

Back on the beach, the sands do shift with the tide. Like sand in the hourglass, when timing is everything, patience is key. Perseverance, though, was not the strong point in this faked drowning scam. The stakes were high, at a $1 million insurance payout from State Farm, but they hadn't banked on having to wait up to twelve years to cash in with no corpse.

This scam began in June 2003, when father of two and one on the way Derek Nicholson[11] had applied for $3 million worth of insurance from State Farm. Despite being unemployed, he falsified his annual income at $80,000 on the application. Regardless of having no occupation, a million-dollar policy was issued on July 22, 2003. His pregnant common-law spouse Nikole Nagle was the named beneficiary.

Within days of the policy issuance, on July 26 of that year, the Tinton Falls, New Jersey pair took their children to the Long Branch Beach, where Derek, wearing only cut-off shorts, went missing in

---

[11] https://www.upi.com/Top_News/2004/05/13/Fraud-charges-laid-in-faked-drowning/71361084466365/

the waves. This was a tragic situation of a young father leaving his family behind.

Pulling in all resources, coast guard boats, a helicopter, and divers were called in for the search and rescue. Obviously devastated by this disastrous twist to their family outing, Nikole and the children returned to the house of Derek's parents, where they had been living, to await news. Days passed, and no sign was recovered.

Nikole gave birth to their third child on July 28.

Within a week, Nikole contacted State Farm to file the claim for life insurance, but she was told nothing would be payable without a body for proof of death. Interestingly enough, she applied for $3 million but was told the policy was for only $1 million.

Amazing coincidence for timing, it's just after this that police in Sea Bright receive an anonymous call stating that a body had been seen floating in the water, which matched the description of Derek Nicholson. Authorities searched, but again, nothing was found. No body recovered. Not a scrap of evidence.

Concerned about this mysterious tip, authorities traced the call. Investigators were able to link the origins of the call to a train in Illinois.

After, it was revealed that part of the couple's plan involved the purchase of two prepaid cells in the names of "Jacob Milsner" and "Michael Way." Under another fictious name, "Anthony Jackson," Derek had prebooked an Amtrak ticket to Los Angeles just days before the vanishing act.

The sands shifted again when, on August 4, Derek was spotted in Manhattan, New York, fully clothed—completely different clothes from those he was wearing when he presumably drowned—and apparently disoriented. When questioned by police, he claimed to be suffering from amnesia.

In May 2004, the couple was arrested on charges of conspiracy to commit insurance fraud, wire fraud, and false distress. They were later found guilty.

As *The Spirit*[12] online newspaper outlined on February 17, 2015, these are what *not* to do when planning to fake your own death:

- Timing—"Dying" less than a week of the policy issuance is suspicious.
- Greed—Wait more than a week before trying to make the insurance claim, especially when there is no corpse.
- Patience—Don't call police yourself to report you've seen your own body floating elsewhere.
- Memory—When staging your reappearance, don't claim amnesia; it's been overused with no results.
- Wardrobe—Staging the reappearance will be more believable if you show up in the same clothes you went missing in.
- Phone logs—Disappearing typically requires going off grid, not maintaining constant contact with traceable phones.
- Other criminal activity—Being suspected of other crimes does not add creditability to the current fictious claim.

---

[12] https://www.westsidespirit.com/news/how-not-to-fake-your-own-death-NYNP1320040525305259990

Hell or High Water ... Maybe Both

Imagine a day perfect for kayaking on the North Sea. The water, as flat as glass, is reflecting the bright, clear sky, blue on blue in the sunshine, with only the thin wedge to distinguish the transition from water to sky on the horizon.

Those were the conditions at 8:00 a.m. on March 21, 2002, when John Darwin,[13] fifty-one, of Seaton Carew, Teesside, United Kingdom, considered it a perfect day to disappear.

John was a prison guard. He wasn't due for work for a few hours, so he took the time for recreation. But when John failed to turn up for his shift at Holme House Prison, Stockton, a massive three-day search-and-rescue operation ensued. The air and sea mission, which stretched from Seaton Carew to Staithes, managed to retrieve only a double-ended paddle for its efforts. The red kayak he'd been seen carrying into the water, which should have been clearly visible on such a day, wouldn't be found until months later where it was discovered smashed at North Gare.

With this kind of evidence, John's family didn't have to wait.

---

[13] https://www.theguardian.com/uk/canoe

John was deemed presumed dead. The death certificate was issued for March 21, 2002, and the insurance money paid to his grieving widow.

How strange then, five years after a portfolio of life insurance policies worth more than £680,000 had been paid to his "widow," that he turned up at a police station, claiming he'd had amnesia this whole time and only managed to find his way home.

At the time of John's disappearance, he and his wife Anne Darwin were in debt well over their heads. Though their children were grown and independent, the couple was drowning from bad investments in real estate, which hadn't created the expected return on investment. Because John was well insured on his life, they hatched a plan to wash out the past and sail on into the future richer than ever.

Some may suggest that the couple all but got away with their apparent fraud, but their downfall in the end seems to be their inability to learn from their mistakes. They simply couldn't refrain from using the insurance proceeds for further investment in real estate, and here is where their story becomes interesting.

Just how did John and Anne manage to sustain the rouse and dupe their children for even five years and leave the country in the process?

After his dip into the North Atlantic, John returned to the family home, where he hid in the couple's adjacent property, leaving everyone, including his two sons, Anthony and Mark, to think him dead. Straight out of Narnia, while his sons grieved next door, according to reports, by day, John would remain in the property hidden, and then at night, he would return to the family home via a secret doorway hidden behind a wardrobe.

This routine continued for four years until John decided to get a passport in the name of a dead baby. From there, the couple made plans to move to South America. Anne related to her sons that, as a widow, she was in need of a new life's start.

Seemingly comfortable in this new life in Panama, in 2004,

John and Anne purchased a two-bedroom apartment and an estate. Finalizing the deal, they posed for a picture with the estate agent. It is not lacking in irony that they intended to build a hotel on the estate, specializing in canoe holidays.

This new life reached a significant speedbump in 2005, when Panamanian authorities changed the residency rule, and John's visa needed to be renewed.

New plan ... easy.

John would just lose any memories of any of the events of the last five years. No one would question a thing because, obviously, he wouldn't be able to remember. In December 2007, John presented himself at a London police station, claiming amnesia. He was able to give his name, date of birth, and personal details but had no idea where he had been all this time.

A lot had, of course, changed in the five years since he'd last been conscious, and with the speed of the World Wide Web, the picture of him and Anne from the year previous surfaced, and a further investigation began. From there, the tidal wave of a storm hit and swamped their stories. On July 23, 2008, John and Anne were each charged with fifteen counts of fraud and money laundering and sentenced to over six years in prison. While John served three years, Anne served three and a half.

John was released in 2011, and the couple divorced. He is said to be living in the Philippines with a new wife.

CHAPTER 15

A Jaws Opportunity or a James Bond Episode of "Never Say Die"

Life gets you down, you're feeling overwhelmed, and you need to clear your head. You go to the shore, look into the great beyond, and wonder what life could be like … if only. Perhaps it's the call of the great horizon or the romance of the sunset on a beautiful day at the beach that seems to be a draw for many looking to cash in on their life insurance policies.

Here, we have John Stonehouse,[14] the son of activist parents and a radical leader in his own right during the 1970s. John experienced a swift rise to political power well into 1970s as a British member of parliament for the Labour Party. During this time, he had been postmaster general and saw the introduction of second-class stamps in 1968. Could it be that he rose too fast and couldn't handle the fame and all its trappings? Some say he fell in with the wrong "sort." Whatever the reasons, on November 20, 1974, while on vacation in Miami, Florida, he left his clothes on a park bench and faked his own death.

---

[14] https://www.bbc.com/news/uk-politics-57942759

What's equally interesting about John Stonehouse is despite the lack of a corpse or any supporting proof, John was presumed drowned and possibly killed by a shark.

However, instead of being fish bait, John had fled the United States. Long before the strict security protocol we're used to today, John used two false identifies he curated long before putting this plan into action and retreated to Australia. There, he took up residence with his mistress, former secretary Sheila Buckley, whom he would later marry.

Under the names of Clive Mildoon and Joe Markham, deceased constituents, John set about transferring large sums of money between banks. Finding the behavior odd, despite not knowing who he was, investigators put him under surveillance. Originally, authorities mistook him for another missing person of equal fame. Calls to Scotland Yard confirmed his correct identity, and the former minister of aviation was arrested Christmas Eve, 1974.

From the moment of his being found, speculation swirled that John had been a Czech spy or that he was being hunted by the mafia. In reality, as with most insurance fraud, it was all financial. At the time of his disappearance, John, husband and father of three, had debts surmounting £$800,000. Prior to his vacation to Florida, he had taken out an insurance policy worth £$170,000. In addition, a charitable fund he'd set up to assist the victims of a Bangladesh hurricane was missing £600,000 from its accounts.

In a trial that lasted sixty-eight days, the Black County politician defended himself against charges of fraud, theft, forgery, conspiracy to defraud, false police investigations, and wasting police time. He claimed he had been blackmailed from South African business partners, and the stress became too much, causing a psychiatric breakdown. This defense held little sway. On August 6, 1976, he was sentenced to Brixton Prison for seven years, to which he served a little less than three because of health issues.

A consummate mover and shaker, after his release, he went on to work as a volunteer fundraiser, wrote three fiction thriller novels, and made numerous television appearances.

John died—for real—in April 1988.

CHAPTER 16

When "Forever" Doesn't Actually Mean F-O-R-E-V-E-R

By all accounts, in 2012, Raymond Roth[15] wanted an escape. Not just to get away from his life, but also his wife. The Long Island, New York man didn't have much going for him. He was an overweight smoker who'd been recently fired from his job, and his marriage was on the rocks. Confiding only to his grown son, he hatched a plan to fake his own death by drowning.

He could have been at his wit's end when he decided it was time for an escape, but instead of booking a vacation, he made plans with his son to fake his own death and collect the insurance payout. Like many before him, he decided that drowning in the ocean would be the easiest way to fake his own death. People drown every year, and the ocean is so big; it would be easy to lose a body.

Downing would be an easy out. For sure, each year there are double-digit drownings from swimming pools, lakes, rivers, and the ocean along the coast. To Raymond, who would question one more?

[15] https://www.latimes.com/nation/la-xpm-2014-mar-04-la-na-nn-fake-drowning-long-island-20140304-story.html

In preparing for his escape, Raymond drafted a new will, increased his life insurance coverage, and proposed the $410,000 in the policy be payable to his son Jonathan. It was later revealed that the plan included that as beneficiary, once in possession of the money, Jonathan would transfer the funds to his father as he built his new life under a new identity elsewhere.

On July 28, 2012, the father and his twenty-two-year-old son Jonathan went to Jones Beach, where Raymond went into the waves by himself, leaving his clothes, wallet, and cell phone behind. Within a half hour, Jonathan called his stepmother Evana to report Raymond missing then made a panicked call to 911, stating his father had been lost in the waves. Playing his role to perfection, he also enlisted the help of on-duty lifeguards to search the beach.

The coast guard and Nassau County Police conducted a search for days to no avail. No body was recovered. However, they did discover that the iPhone had been wiped clean of all data and found it interesting that Raymond's driver's license had gone missing from his wallet.

Completely unaware of the plan, Raymond's wife Evana then discovered their bank accounts had been emptied. Motivated into action, digging deeper, she then found e-mails between Raymond and his son outlining the details of the plan, including how they would communicate once Raymond made his escape. She immediately reported the scheme to police.

Within a week, Raymond was spotted at his timeshare in West Gate Lake Resort in Orlando, Florida. Then he was spotted again when he received a speeding ticket in South Carolina.

Once captured, he went on to plead guilty to insurance fraud in March 2013 and was ordered to pay more than $36,000 in restitution for the emergency's services, search and rescue, police presence, and helicopters involved in the search for a lost swimmer from Jones Beach. Although Jonathan pleaded not guilty to his part, claiming he'd been coerced, the court found him guilty, and he too served time.

TRAVELING

When the Destination
Is Not the Beach

CHAPTER 17

Pack Your Bags, We Off for Some Travel Insurance Fraud

Emergency out-of-country medical, otherwise known as travel insurance, is typically purchased to protect the insured against a risk of loss. This loss can include the risk of not being able to travel, the risk of losing their bags and belongings while traveling, or something happening, typically a medical situation, to them while out of the country. The policies are purchased from private insurance underwriters through licensed agents.

However, there continues to be a significant amount of fraud from bogus policies from nonexistent insurers sold by unlicensed agents to medical practitioners making false claims for insurance proceeds for injuries never sustained.

From claiming for missing baggage that didn't exist in the first place to claiming for a trip cancelation when it is a nonmedical reason, exaggerating injuries for more money, the list is lengthy.

On one hand, you have George Fredrickson,[16] who never suspected that the $432 travel insurance policy he purchased for his

---

[16] https://www.cnn.com/2009/TRAVEL/traveltips/04/07/travel.insurance.scams/

$8,000 transatlantic cruise was fake. It was only when he needed to file a claim for cancelation insurance, through Traveler Protection Services, that he discovered the policy was a fake. Not only did he lose going on the trip, but he also lost the value as well because of no insurance.

Then we have Ayodele Salako, who we don't know if he ever even went on a trip. However, he certainly knew how to make a travel insurance claim through his legitimate travel insurer.

It can be said Ayodele went from the frying pan into the fryer, quite literally in this fraudulent scheme. This United Kingdom resident used a frying pan receipt as evidence of a $2,000 bogus travel insurance claim and found himself jailed for fraud.

The claim stated that Ayodele had been robbed on his way to Heathrow Airport. In his bag was apparently four mobile phones, two laptops, and clothing. In addition to not being able to prove he actually owned the items listed, never mind the bag, he couldn't verify he'd had an actual flight booked.

When the insurer became suspicious, they referred the claim to the Insurance Fraud Enforcement Department based out of London Police. Ayodele was charged with false representation, where he pleaded guilty, and sentenced to a trip he likely didn't count on—six weeks in jail. No baggage check.

CHAPTER 18

Serial Fraud Is Not a Business Plan

Theodore Robert Wright III[17] had the persona of a jet-setting, risk-taking millionaire businessman. At least that's what his social media feeds reflected. The feed included a fascinating life of adventure. He made himself known as someone who took part in risky business schemes, arms dealing, and landing planes in dangerous situations and always coming out on top. Perhaps what was less well known was his habit of destroying luxury cars, boats, and planes from the Pacific to the Gulf of Mexico in an effort to collect on the insurance.

For this convicted insurance fraudster, he made loss, damage, and personal injury insurance claims to various carriers, including State Farm, Catlin Insurance, Old Republic Aerospace Inc., and Progressive Insurance, to name a few.

While it's not uncommon to insure luxury items for more than the purchased price, Theodore was making a profitable living off destroying extravagant vehicles and collecting the insurance payout.

---

[17] https://www.texasmonthly.com/news-politics/it-was-never-enough/

This seems to have kicked off back in March 2012, when Theodore purchased a 1966 Beechcraft Baron plane for $46,000 and insured it for almost double the market price at $85,000. Only one year after purchasing the craft, Theodore crashed the plane somewhere in the Gulf of Mexico. The plane was conveniently never recovered, but Theodore and his friend Raymond Fosdick managed to salvage a waterproof iPad that they used to film themselves in the middle of the ocean, waiting to be rescued. This video eventually made its way to the Internet, where Theodore garnered national attention. What was most notable about this video is how calm Theodore and Raymond seemed to be after what was supposedly a traumatizing and unexpected plane crash.

As if getting paid $39,000 for crashing a plane wasn't enough, Fosdick proceeded to sue Theodore for personal injury to the tune of $1 million. While the lawsuit was eventually settled by the insurance carrier for $100,000, it was later discovered that at least some of that money was then transferred to one of Theodore's companies.

Between the plane and the lawsuit, Theodore was making some decent money, but this was just the beginning. In 2013, Theodore bought a salvaged 2008 Lamborghini Gallardo for $76,000, which was insured as if it was brand new. When he crashed and flooded it, he earned $169,554 on the insurance payout.

Only a few months after crashing his new car, Theodore purchased a 1971 Cessna 500 Citation aircraft for $190,000. Despite being grounded for two weeks, Theodore's new plane went up in flames at Athens, Texas airport in 2014. The craft was insured for $440,000, which was paid in full because of the loss.

Planes aren't exactly known for bursting into flames when left unattended on the tarmac, which is why it should come as no surprise that this was the first of Theodore's "accidents" that caught the attention of the Bureau of Alcohol, Tobacco, Firearms, and Explosives. Subsequent investigations were also conducted by the

FAA Law Enforcement Assistance Program, the Texas Department of Insurance, and the National Insurance Crime Bureau.

Clearly, Theodore needed to come up with more elaborate schemes than just crashing his cars or lighting his planes on fire if he was going to evade authorities. So in October 2014, not long after the Cessna tarmac barbecue, Theodore bought a 1998 Hunter Passage yacht for $50,150. Instead of sinking this boat himself, Theodore sold the boat to a man in Honolulu for $193,500. The Honolulu man bought the boat with a loan Theodore had supplied to him through a mortgage company Theodore had created. The vessel was sunk in 2016 in a Ko O'lina, Hawaiian marina, and the $180,023 in insurance proceeds were paid in full.

Despite Theodore's more sophisticated methods of committing insurance fraud, the feds eventually uncovered his schemes, and in the summer of 2017, Theodore was arrested in Nevada by the US Marshall Service. In his first court appearance, Theodore was represented by Gabriel Grasso, one of the lawyers who had also represented O. J. Simpson.

In December 2017, Theodore pleaded guilty to conspiracy to commit arson and conspiracy to commit wire fraud. Theodore was sentenced to sixty-five months in federal prison and had to pay $988,554 in restitution. However, one article suggested Theodore claimed he had accumulated more than $35 million in fraudulent insurance claims around the world, though none of that has been proven.

Theodore Wright is set to be released from his sentence in February 2022.

ZOOM ZOOM

Pedal to the Metal

CHAPTER 19

Auto Insurance—Operation Sledgehammer

f there's a road and automobiles able to drive upon it, then there's likely been an accident as well.

Traffic collisions are as commonplace as the roads themselves. According to the *Association for Safe International Road Travel*,[18] there are more than 1.35 million deaths globally caused by motorway crashes every year. That adds up to a whopping 3,700 deaths each and every day just from vehicle accidents.

Where there are cars and collisions, there is also auto insurance because the economic impact to Americans alone is more than $871 billion, with roughly $380 million in direct medical costs.

Auto insurance is required by law to operate a vehicle in most places and will usually cover the costs associated with traffic collisions, including covering the medical costs of those involved in the accident. But with so many collisions happening every day, it has created an opportunity for criminals and crime organizations to see an opportunity for insurance fraud.

---

[18] https://www.asirt.org

This is the story of when those "calamities" are no longer "unforeseen" but instead "planned" and "curated" events.

Purported to perhaps be the largest and most sophisticated auto insurance fraud to date was "Operation Sledgehammer." "Operation Sledgehammer"[19] was the name for a South Florida ring of conspirators responsible for more than $20 million in fraudulent claims between 2006 and 2012. These fraudsters would stage accidents by destroying a car with a sledgehammer, hence the name, and bring people on to act as victims of the collision. These people would go to chiropractor clinics owned by the ringleaders of this operation and fake injuries. All the medical professionals at these clinics were involved in this scheme and would submit false claims to the insurance companies.

Many times, if not most times, for an insurance fraud this complex to be successful, there needs to be collusion. This is an agreement between multiple parties to take advantage of another party to gain a profit illegally.

This scheme required a lot of people. The ring consisted of at least ninety-two people who worked at the treatment facilities, worked as medical professionals, or who owned the clinics. The people who owned the clinics were, of course, stand-ins for the ring leaders of this operation. "Operation Sledgehammer" also employed several recruiters to scout out people to act as the victims of fake collisions. These recruiters would also teach the victims about staging and claiming practices, including how to file police reports. These individuals were paid once the claims were filed and the ring leaders received the money.

Behind some of the biggest scams are organized operations that first set out to prey on the more venerable members of society and sometimes give them no choice but to patriciate. This could be because they are in a country illegally. Perhaps they are poor and will

---

[19] https://abc7ny.com/car-insurance-fraud-operation-sledgehammer-jawahir-enterprise-sledhammer/8637346/

grasp any straw for an income. This does not excuse them from the crime but is said simply to set the context.

Staging was another essential key to the success of this conspiracy. Investigators codenamed the operation "sledgehammer" because the participants were taught how to use the mighty tool to inflict the correct amount of damage on their vehicle to defraud the insurance system. The vehicle had to have the right look if they were going to pull this off. You couldn't have an untouched paint job, and you couldn't just create damage anywhere. This had to be strategically choreographed.

Defendants from Palm Beach, Broward, and Miami-Dade counties in Florida were charged in this massive scheme. From fake aches and pains to duplicitous diagnosis and treatment plans, falsified bills for these services, the ring leaders had devised a complicated plan that would, to some, rival any well-organized legitimate business recognized by *Fortune* magazine. They even had recruiters to source "victims" and train them on staging and claiming practices, including how to file police reports.

Multiple charges, including mail fraud, money laundering, structuring financial transactions, and participating in staged-accident fraud, among others, were filed. The list is long.

Like a well-oiled machine, the five key players used the US mail in their scheme to take advantage of the Personal Injury Protection (PIP) of auto insurance. They seemed to know exactly what they wanted to happen, even ensuring that all claimed reimbursements were paid into controlled accounts where they would then pay the participants once the money was received, much like a commission for job well done.

How did it all work?

Licensed chiropractors served as "named owners" of clinics, leaving the leaders in financial control. Then recruiters sourced real or fake auto accident victims' treatment, real or imagined, at the clinics. Injury "victims" were referred to as "Perro" and "Perra" or

"Macho" and "Hembra." The next and most essential step was to bill the insurance carriers for reimbursement based on "injuries" without co-pays or deductibles. This would involve knowledge of how to file these claims correctly to ensure they would be paid without hassle.

Those charged included the ring leaders, two of which are said to have fled to Cuba, licensed chiropractors, massage therapists, health care providers, complicit clinic employees, bogusly injured accident participants, which included one mother who actually involved her five children.

CHAPTER 20

Ten Gets You Fifteen Plus Prison

People who understand the process of filing an insurance claim, the ins and outs of what is involved, are sometimes the culprits. This is the case in this little switcharoo from someone who should have known better because they knew how to. Here, we feature Suliman Kamara,[20] who, one would assume, not only would know better, but also would have been expected to prevent such dealings.

All for the sake of a little more than $10,000 from a Liberty Mutual insurance claim, Suliman, now an ex-police officer, faced jail time and up to $15,000 in fines. Additionally, for someone in the position of authority, this is a great example of "What were you thinking?"

In 2009, Newark, New Jersey police officer Suliman reported his sport utility vehicle stolen. To add insult to injury, he, in fact, had filed the false claim through his own department. Perhaps because

---

[20] https://www.nj.com/somerset/2014/02/ex-newark_cop_sentenced_to_probation_for_falsely_reporting_stolen_car_collecting_10k_in_insurance_mo.html

of this, the insurance company paid the claim in full, no further questions asked, assuming the SUV was irretrievable.

Kamara's claim not only considered the supposed value for the loss of the vehicle, but also for costs of purported property inside and the expense of a rental car.

Some may suggest this was a bold move when after accepting the payout for the loss, Kamara continued to drive the car for an additional three years. The only change he made to the 2003 GMC Yukon to cover the offense was to change the license plate. After three years, he very likely he assumed he'd gotten away with the scam and may have, if not for a Liberty Mutual insurance representative who noticed the car parked in Kamara's driveway as he drove past himself on the way home from work.

For this offense, Kamara pleaded guilty to theft by deception.

But the depth of his deception, especially as a person in a position of trust, didn't end there, and this kind of record-tampering was not the end of his offenses. Added to the insurance fraud, Kamara had federal charges pending, claiming that, along with his spouse Sameerah Lee, he conspired to obtain more than $60,000 in benefits under section 8 of the public housing assistance program.

To collect from the housing assistance program, Kamara and his wife filed false documents and did not disclose to the Newark Housing Authority that they lived together. This, thereby, ensured Kamara's income would not be considered in determining whether Lee qualified for benefits.

CHAPTER 21

Good Intentions or Golden Opportunity

Rev the engines, it's time to put the rubber to the road. Some may call this a joy ride gone bad. Others may suggest a good reprimand was in order. However things started, they certainly escalated into something completely different.

In December 2009, Mohammed Kayes[21] was seventeen. Despite not having a valid driver's license, he and his friends took his mother's car without permission. As luck would have it, they were involved in a car accident.

Mohammed's father Louay Kayes, along with his uncle Hassan Nazir Kaiss, arrived on the scene ahead of the police. Once there, all parties decided that Louay would claim responsibility for the operation of the vehicle when filing the report with the authorities. The car was insured under a policy issued by Traders General Insurance Co.

Interesting, despite knowing who the original operator of the

---

[21] https://torontosun.com/news/local-news/mandel-brothers-ordered-to-pay-200gs-for-deliberate-insurance-scam

vehicle was and who was responsible for the accident, the driver of the other vehicle said nothing as the false statements were entered.

Shortly thereafter, this Ontario father began entering claims to the insurance company for injuries sustained as a result of being involved in the accident, an accident for which he had had no physical presence. For the next year, Louay attended and received treatments from Metro Rehabilitation Centre and Assessment Direct Inc., where he claimed well over $43,000. Additional claims were filed for housekeeping, home maintenance, caregiving, attendant care, etc., amounting to close to $40,000. A final settlement was issued from the insurer for $19,000 and roughly $8,000 more for repairs to his car.

Where things seemed to fall apart in this scam was when Louay's brother Hassan sued Louay for $1 million in personal damages for injuries he suggested he received as a fictitious passenger in a vehicle accident he was never present. Both brothers went along with the tale to the insurers and the lawyers.

It was only in 2014, when the other driver finally came forward to Traders Insurance, that action against Louay and two others was taken for fraud and conspiracy.

The court found Traders was entitled to $118,109 in restitution. No other criminal charges were laid. While the court refused to award punitive damages against Louay and Hassan, they further removed the charges against Mohammed, stating there was a wide gap between the available evidence and conclusion that Mohammed was in on the intended fraud.

In the end, the court ordered that compensatory damages and costs would more than adequately serve to punish defendants' misconduct.

CHAPTER 22

What the Duff?

We actually may know this person. First, it starts with the recreational vehicle stolen, trailer and all, from right in front of the house just after nightfall. Then only a year later, there's the truck that spontaneously caught fire on the road in front of the house in broad daylight with all the contents inside. What a loss. But wait, the very next year another truck is stolen from a shed, full of supposed valuables, yet the shop with all the tools of the trade were left untouched. What luck.

Over and over, surveys[22] suggest that people not only accept insurance fraud as a "norm," but also, many would participate given the right situation. "Participation," as it turns out, takes many forms, whether as an organizer, the actual perpetrator, a conspirator on the sidelines as part of collusion, or someone who turns a blind eye.

Like the example given, it could be the perpetual "bad luck" scenario, or the adjuster who doesn't question further, or those in the "know" who shake their head and say, "Well, what can I do about

---

[22] https://www.bloomberg.com/press-releases/2018-12-04/aviva-fraud-report-2018-majority-of-ontarians-believe-25-of-claims-are-fraudulent

it anyhow?" Little wonder then that it is estimated that insurance fraud in the latter teens of the 2000s amounted to more than $1.6 billion annually in Canada alone, $40 billion in the United States.

As infrequent as it may seem to the outsider, there are those who continuously hunt and prosecute fraud, looking for the signs, building their sting, and taking action.

One such contributing fraud launched the first of its kind, undercover insurance investigation in Canada. Toronto Police launched the "Project Duffy"[23] task force to unravel a phony car accident injury racket. This planned swindle involved not only your average taxpaying Canadian, but health and legal professionals as well.

Here's how the fraud would typically play out: Participants seeking phony claims would go to the clinic and sign a sheet for unnecessary multiple treatments for which they had needed to attend. The Wellness Centres would then send a bill to the insurer for services as though they were required and received. All that really happened was paperwork was submitted and money received.

Ante were first raised when an Aviva-insured person came forward in 2014, stating they no longer wanted to file their legitimate insurance claim. Brows furrowed because in this case, the car had been totalled, but there was no collision insurance. This meant that although they couldn't file a claim for the damage to their vehicle, they could claim for injuries sustained and treated. For this person, a friend had suggested that they knew a place where they could get the money even though they weren't entitled to any insurance. This was when the insured was introduced to the Wellness Centres of Ontario.

Via months of video surveillance and undercover protocol, in March 2016, police were able to file charges against chiropractor Dr. Edward Hayes of Vaughan and Doina Osacenco of Toronto,

---

[23] https://www.thestar.com/news/crime/2012/02/23/car_insurance_scam_37_arrested_in_project_whiplash_raids.html

both employed by the Wellness Centres of Ontario, and Thornhill resident Anna Kovtanuka, a paralegal of Kovtman Law in Toronto.

As a consequence, Edward Hayes issued a guilty plea to one count of fraud under $5,000. For this, he received a six-month conditional sentence and a twelve-month probation order. The College of Chiropractors of Ontario (CCO) initially suspended Dr. Hayes's chiropractor license. Then in late 2017, the college completed a review and found that Dr. Hayes committed eight counts of professional misconduct.

Michelle Osacenco pleaded guilty to one count of fraud under $5,000 and received a conditional discharge, a twelve-month probation order, and a $1,500 freestanding restitution order.

Pleading guilty to one count of attempted fraud under $5,000, Anna Kovtanuka received a conditional discharge, a three-year probation order, and a $1,000 freestanding restitution order. On November 20, 2017, her paralegal license was revoked by the Law Society of Ontario.

The Wellness Centres of Ontario were issued an order to cease operations by the Financial Services Commission of Ontario. They were required to pay an administrative monetary penalty of $21,985.17, and clinic owner Tatiana Amelian received an additional administrative monetary penalty of $4,000.

It has been suggested the clinic simply reopened under a new name.

CHAPTER 23

Swoop and Squat—What?

Who's the next victim in this crime ring?

Imagine driving and unbeknownst to you, your vehicle has been targeted. Suddenly, you're run off the road to deliberately create an accident. Try to wrap your head around two parties being involved, and you happen to be an innocent bystander dragged into the crash—by no fault of your own. This is what auto insurance investigators call the "swoop and squat" maneuver ran by highly sophisticated criminal rings.

It's called the "swoop and squat"[24] maneuver because one car "swoops" in front of the target and the other will drive to the side to ensure the victim cannot swerve out of the way. The "squat" is when the "swoop" car jams the breaks to create a rear-end. This fraud operation will either involve making false injury claims after the "accident" or scamming the victim into thinking they are at fault and paying the restitution.

Unfortunately, there isn't one particular locale where this happens. Nor is this trick confined to one country or another. The

---

[24] https://www.4autoinsurancequote.com/swoop-and-squat-auto-insurance-fraud/

scam works so well everywhere, it has become common place for investigators who know the signs.

To an onlooker, the accident looks credible. Sometimes there are even fatalities. But the conspirators have been roped in for payment, likely never knowing the actual risks to body and person.

From the early 1990s, marginalized people, poor immigrants, and those in need of cash have been targeted by multitiered criminal organizations to participate. Usually, at the top of the organization, there are professional lawyers and doctors who profit by false diagnosis of injuries and legal claims. These organizations invest in vehicles that are just drivable as their only function is to be destroyed in the planned "accident." As a precaution, to help protect the participants, in which there could be as many as four per "crash" vehicle, the conspirators will load items in the trunk to cushion from the expected crash.

Their victims, by contrast, never see this coming. There is no preparation. Serious bodily harm does happen.

Typically, the collaborators will target commercial or expensive model vehicles, which would likely be well insured, as they are looking for large payouts. The plan would die in conception if they target uninsured or under-insured autos. The next step involves the accomplices to the crime picking a location where there would be no witnesses to provide conflicting reports. Again, to pull off the caper, all records need to be in order. Once the "accident" is carried out, preconceived stories are delivered to the authorities, and then the claims start. From soft tissue to whiplash, sprains, brakes, etc., the claims are filed through the various professions for authenticity.

In many cases, when the damage hasn't been significant enough and people are not injured, the scammers will turn to their prey and further victimize them to get their money. After the event, they make the crash look as though the target is at fault. This is the part of the scam that involves convincing the person to settle out of court to avoid the dreaded increased insurance fees and legal costs.

Unfortunately, this is yet another part of the plan. After they strike the agreement, within days, the victim is notified that there will, in fact, be claims from the accident brought about by injuries sustained by all parties in the vehicles.

Now the victim, seen to be at fault because there were no witnesses, will be made to pay again through higher premiums.

CHAPTER 24

The Devil Is in the Details

Or perhaps there are no details at all. Certainly, when James Kalfsbeek[25] took the wheel of this business, incorporated in British Columbia, Canada, operating in California, he seemed to put Christ in charge. Or at least in the title.

James, a self-avowed sovereign citizen and Christian, decided he was going to create his own kind of insurance. In 1994, James founded the Puget's Sound Agricultural Society, also known as the *Jesus Christ Administrators*. This organization created their own kind of auto insurance that was not regulated or legal. It was sold as a membership and as a legitimate alternative to regular auto insurance. Despite the numerous cease-and-desist orders issued by insurance-regulating authorities, the Jesus Christ Administrators assured their clients that the coverage issued was in compliance with state law.

Working within the realm of "organic Christian people," Puget's Sound Agricultural Society began to issue lifetime memberships for a fee of $500, plus a lifetime fee of $250 per vehicle. For this,

---

[25] https://archives.fbi.gov/archives/sacramento/press-releases/2009/sc061109.htm

participants were issued insurance identification cards, confirming they would be covered for any automotive accidents so long as the accident was not as a result of alcohol. Additionally, if there was any bodily injury, primarily pain and suffering, there would be no coverage payable as that was considered part of "God's plan."

Above and beyond the inherent misfortune that comes with fraudulent coverage like this, clients who reported their accidents to the authorities would have their license's suspended because of not having legal insurance, this despite members, primarily in California, being reassured that the coverage was in compliance with that state's law.

Unbelievably, between 1996 and 2002, Puget's Sound Agricultural Society collected millions of dollars in fees, which was retained in a Canadian bank. However, when auto claims were incurred and submitted for recovery, the company chose to assess the claim after the fact and decided independently which claimants would be paid and which would not. It is unclear how those additional funds for payment were established from the members. While most smaller claims were honored, the larger ones were not.

The additional burden of license suspension often accompanied the wreck for participants because when they reported the collision to the authorities, they were found to be not in possession of real insurance. For this, they had to pay the penalty of getting their driving rights re-established.

In the end, not only did Puget's Sound Agricultural Society defraud their own members, but they also flagrantly operated in violation of state department of motor vehicles and law enforcement. Sadly, as in one circumstance, when a member was involved in a devastating car accident, which resulted in a death and grievous injury, the Jesus Christ Administrators claimed not to have to pay the $20 million from a Michigan court judgment. And even when they did finally agree to pay, they issued a bogus financial document called a "Bill of Exchange."

Sentenced in August 2009, James and others associated with this international insurance fraud were convicted for conspiracy, mail fraud, wire fraud, and money laundering.

James received ten-year jail time.

CHAPTER 25

These Students May Have Been Better Off to "Fake" a Grade

M akes you wonder how far some students will go for a "pass." Pass someone to write your report, perhaps even take the test, hack the computer system, and change the grades ... that's small time compared to this installment.

Darwin Arias and Roger Luna[26] were Aldine Senior High School teenagers failing chemistry when their teacher Tramesha Lashon Fox offered them passing grades if they agreed to steal and then torch her car.

Although there is not one chemical formula for fire, flames, typically, are made up of carbon dioxide, water, vapor, oxygen, and nitrogen, and these two seemed to have no trouble accommodating the request. Of course, had they relied upon the math, they may have rethought their decisions.

By the time Tramesha had convinced the two to be her accomplices, she had already replaced the 2003 Chevrolet Malibu with a

[26] https://buffalonews.com/news/arson-insurance-fraud-alleged-against-teacher/article_6b098798-4785-5b72-8380-473af7cf45da.html

2005 Toyota Corolla. Behind on her payments by three months and facing repossession, she wanted to cash on the insurance money and avoid the $20,000 still owing on the older vehicle. So on the last day of school, May 27, as directed, the two students took the unlocked car from the shopping mall where they were told it would be and drove it to a wooded area, which happened to be fairly close to one of their homes, and set it ablaze.

While Tramesha reported the car stolen to authorities that very same day, it was twelve more days before the torched car was found not far from Darwin's home. In the meantime, for their efforts, Darwin received a 90 for end-of-term grade and Roger an 80. In addition, they were charged with arson. To avoid jail time, they entered plea deals and were granted deferred adjudication, probation, community service, and required to pay restitution.

For her part, Tramesha faced felony arson and insurance fraud. Future car payments were likely hard to keep up on as she was fired from her job and served ninety days in jail.

WHERE THERE'S SMOKE,

There's an Opportunity for Insurance Fraud

CHAPTER 26

What Not to Do in a "Buyer's" Market

Technically, fire is the rapid oxidation of materials. Flammable materials are referred to as the "fuel" in the chemical process of combustion. And that's about as much information most people have when they decide to light the match. A strong blaze is also a common scapegoat for those looking to cash in on their insurance.

Clearly, Victor and Olga Barriere[27] gave little thought to the repercussions of assigning such a task to their repair and maintenance contractor. What more would you need to know?

Every situation seems justified in the beginning. Certainly, relatable. Going back to July 2007, in Long Beach, California, Victor and Olga were struggling. They had a $315,000 mortgage on their six-hundred-square-foot 1921 home. In addition, to maintain the property to code, they had to fund the repairs and residential upkeep. Expenses were mounting. They tried unsuccessfully to sell

---

[27] https://www.insurancebusinessmag.com/au/news/breaking-news/far-out-friday-the-silliest-false-insurance-claims-revealed-54205.aspx

many times until there seemed only one way out—burn the place down and collect what they could on the insurance.

Of course, it seems the first rule to any insurance fraud is to not get caught. Put distance between you and the crime and come up with an alibi to maintain your innocence. So Victor and Olga hired Thomas Trucios, a local handyman, to do the job for them. They gave him the instruction to torch the place. The problem was that although Thomas accepted the job, he was ill prepared in the art of arson. This was, by all accounts, his first foray into this criminal activity, and having no prior experience in arson and in using too much gasoline, he caused a massive explosion.

Unbeknownst to Thomas, in his preparation, fuel fumes had built to dangerous levels. Ignorant of the ramifications, he proceeded to use significant qualities of gasoline. Then when he lit the flame, Thomas wasn't far enough away to protect him from the TNT-like blast, which blew out the windows, cracked the pavement, and woke the neighborhood for several blocks.

Despite the third-degree burns to more than 95 percent of his body, Thomas managed to phone his wife and get into his car. When she met him, kids in tow, she transferred him into her car and rushed him to USC Medical Center, where he later died.

Despite proving in court that they had no intention of killing Thomas, Victor and Olga were charged with involuntary man-slaughter, conspiracy to commit arson, and conspiracy to commit insurance fraud. While Victor was sentenced to fourteen years, Olga was sentenced to six years behind bars.

Interestingly, three years after the tragedy, the vacant lot sold for US$30,000.

* * *

Of course, the Barrieres aren't the only ones to find their best-laid plans go up tragically in smoke. One of the largest fires in the city of Toronto's history was an insurance fraud.

The Woodbine Building Supply store was owned by John Magno and his two brothers Frank and Carlo. The store had been a staple in the city's east end of Danforth Avenue since their father first opened the store. But in 2001, Woodbine, having issues remaining competitive against the local Home Depot, John often found himself up against local community criticism. On one such occasion, the business had been fined $11,800 for improper storage of materials.

The brothers had decided to move locations and start fresh. In its place, once they cleared the site and removed the old Woodbine building, they would construct a condo development. In preparation, the brothers increased their insurance on the store and received a $145,000 demolition quotation to clear the lot. This was rejected.

Instead, on Christmas Eve, five accomplices were hired to remove all existing merchandise, said to amount to close to a million dollars, and set the building aflame so the insurance money could be collected without incurring demolition fees. The conspirators included fellow Toronto businessman Adrian Roks Jr.; John "Sam" Paskalis, a local con artist; Tony Jarcevic, a student of fire prevention at the local community college; Shaun McMaster, driver; and Jason Regaldo, who would store the stolen goods.

Because of the location in the heart of the residential community of Danforth, the group chose Christmas Eve as it was felt the local Italian and Greek families would be safely away at church. While the others removed the merchandise, Tony and Sam set to work spreading gasoline and fertilizer in the basement. Sam left when the fumes got to be too much, but when the first attempt to light the place up failed, Tony called Sam back. The resulting explosion occurred, just after midnight and supposedly accidentally when the flammable vapors ignited. This caused Sam to be severely burned and hospitalized. Tony was killed in the blast, and his body not recovered for seventeen days.

Close to two hundred fire fighters and dozens of trucks were called to the scene to control the inferno, which displaced fifty nearby homes and caused more than $4 million in damages.

Shortly after, John filed an insurance claim for $3.5 million.

John Magno was sentenced to twelve years in prison for manslaughter and arson. The accomplices were also charged and sentenced in varying degrees.

The site sat empty for many years until JFC Properties, owned by John, Frank, and Carlo Magno built Carmelina Condominiums. This twelve-story development, featuring 148 residential units and street-level retail, was completed in 2015.

CHAPTER 27

Who Would Know Better Than an Adjuster?

Aptly named "Operation Flames and Flood,"[28] this case involved a conspiracy led by a public adjustor business owner Jorge Fausto Espinosa out of Florida. In his "arson for hire" scam, he managed to defraud approximately fourteen insurance companies out of $14 million in fake and inflated claims.

Enlisting the help of the homeowner, he set fire or flooded homes to claim on the insurance. Sentenced to twenty years in jail, Jorge and his cohorts caused at least twenty-eight cases of arson in South Florida—the Miami-Dade, Lee, and Collier counties. The scene was set to look as though the house had electrical problems, suffered a kitchen accident, or had faulty waterlines.

So much for nationwide adjusters, Jorge pleaded guilty to racketeering, racketeering conspiracy, organized scheme to defraud, arson, insurance fraud, and grand theft. Additionally, he was ordered to pay $1.9 million in restitution.

---

[28] https://www.citizensfla.com/documents/20702/121545/20150604+Operation+Flames+and+Floods+II%3B+More.pdf/49559021-b75f-4c42-9b21-75c2dbe-76a7b?version=1.0&t=1447776546887&download=true

CHAPTER 28

When Arson and Murder Combine

According to United States National Fire Protection Association,[29] fire departments respond to an average of 346,800 fires annually. Between 2015 and 2019, more than a quarter of fires occur in the home caused primarily from cooking, followed by heating, electrical, smoking, and then intentionally set blazes; 75 percent of these resulting in death.

Focusing on the deliberately set burns, we can surmise many of these are set with a financial windfall in mind. To burn down your home to collect on the insurance money is fraud. To purposefully leave your own mom in the basement to die and make it look like she did it as a suicide attempt is criminal. So the courts determined.

At first, Marc Thompson[30] seemed to have gotten away with the deed. However, it may have seemed odd that the fifty-four-year-old former commodities executive, who earned a cool million, hid

---

[29] https://www.nfpa.org
[30] https://caselaw.findlaw.com/us-7th-circuit/1459489.html

a portion of the insurance payout in an offshore account and then filed for bankruptcy.

Here's how it is said to have gone down. On August 11, 2002, Marc used a lacquer thinner as an accelerant. This was poured along the wall. He then led his ninety-year-old mother, Carmen Thompson, to the basement prior to lighting the fire starter. At first, authorities said Carmen died by carbon monoxide poisoning and smoke inhalation, which led to the ruling of her death as suicide.

After the house was torched, where Marc claimed his mother set the blaze to hide his own copiability and create an alibi, he quickly claimed $730,000 in insurance money. In what prosecutors said was an attempt to hide and perhaps safeguard the proceeds, he then set up a shell corporation in the Republic of Mauritius, an island in the Indian Ocean.

Mauritius stands approximately two thousand kilometers off the southeast coast of Africa, not far from Madagascar. An independent nation since 1965, Mauritius may have been chosen because of its exclusive economic zone and the fact that it is classified by the World Bank as a high-income economy. It was there that Marc laundered $400,000 and then claimed insolvency in May 2003 to escape his other lingering debts.

Because of federal prosecution, Marc was not charged with murder; however, he was convicted of nineteen felony charges, including arson to commit insurance and bankruptcy fraud. So much for high living for this former grain futures executive, Marc was sentenced to 190 years in federal prison.

COMMERCIAL INSURANCE

Name Your Fraud

CHAPTER 29

When the Bungee Cord Snaps Back

While the purchase of commercial insurance is not compulsory, many businesses will have some insurance to cover them in the event of a loss, especially if they have outstanding loans with their bank. This could be to insure the property, contents, corporately owned vehicles, any form of liability from being sued, from customers to employees alike. There's also insurance for when the business can't operate from situations outside their control. Many times we can use the example of natural disasters, like fire, flood, tornados, etc.

General liability coverage may assist when the operation is sued. This could be from a slip-and-fall, product-related mishap, etc.

When underwriters place the policy, they will look at the type of business, the physical premises, the tools and/or equipment, intellectual property, employees, and customers. In this, insurer may assign the policy based on nature of the industry, like retail, restaurants, landscapers, accountants, and the list goes on.

Yes, there is even coverage for circuses and their performers.

Illinois businessman Richard Brooks[31] owned and operated Richard A. Brooks & Associates Ltd. out of his home. Neither a licensed agent, broker, nor insurer, he'd held no contracts to sell insurance with any insurance company since 1997. This, however, did not deter Richard from creating a niche market for himself by targeting amusement parks, circuses, zoos, and extreme sport facilities for his fictitious Lloyd's of London coverage.

All over the United States, Richard sold bogus certificates of insurance to operators of carnivals, bungee-jumping sports, rock-climbing, mechanical bulls, and other performance-based establishments. Problems arose in May 2005, when a petting zoo in Florida tried to file their claim with Lloyd's of London and were declined. Lloyd's indicated they had never issued such a certificate and, further, had never heard of Richard or his company.

Officials in Nebraska and Kentucky performed a series of routine inspections of amusement parks, requesting proof of insurance in the process. In the process, they reconfirmed with Lloyd's of London that the certificates were not authentic.

It is a blessing and a curse that many of those who purchased insurance through Richard never had to file a claim and, therefore, had not suffered financially; however, for those who did, they only found out after their claim was declined that they, in fact, had insurance.

Richard pleaded guilty to selling more than two hundred fake policies. Included in the plea was an acknowledgment of nine counts of theft over $100,000 mail fraud, resulting in more than $2.9 million in fraud. Richard was sentenced to seven and a half years in prison.

---

[31] https://www.oakpark.com/2007/01/04/rf-man-convicted-in-insurance-scam/

CHAPTER 30

When Thrills Turn to Spills

Here's what happened when you run, what some people termed, the most dangerous amusement park in North America, or at least New Jersey, and are required to carry insurance but no carrier will take the risk.

Go to the Cayman Islands, open a "paper-based" insurance carrier, and name it London and World Assurance Ltd.[32] Then issue yourself some nonexistent insurance to get the state authorities off your back.

Always a risk-taker, in the 1970s, Eugene "Gene" Mulvihill[33] started on Wall Street at the height of the penny stocks to make his fortune. Also known as the "pump and dump" for their worthlessness, he and partner Robert Brennan operated Mayflower Securities until being suspended in 1973. That was when he and some other investors formed a company called Great American Recreation and purchased Vernon Valley/Great George ski resort located fifty miles northeast of New York City in Vernon, New Jersey. The added

[32] https://www.datocapital.ky/companies/London-%26-World-Assurance-Ltd.html
[33] https://www.menshealth.com/entertainment/a33796023/gene-mulvilhill-action-park-hbo-max/

benefit of the purchase was that it also housed the exclusive Great George Playboy Club.

This was lucrative in the winter, but it left the summer without a revenue stream until, in the summer of 1976, the group decided to construct Action Park. Not one for following any rules, it seems this waterpark/amusement area would leave a legacy of stories so crazy they had to be true that to leave the park without any injury meant you couldn't have partaken of any of the rides.

From inexperienced, untrained teenage operators to drunk and disorderly behavior from patrons and staff alike, open drug use and sexual activity were common. Gene was a true believer in anyone agreeing to come to the park, consenting to the rides, were ultimately responsible for any injuries. Those who worked at the park followed suit. Catastrophes ensued, including lacerations, concussions, bruising, cuts, broken bones, chipped teeth, and deaths.

No surprise, Action Park earned the reputation as the most insane park in existence with stories circulated that a test dummy came out of one of the rides headless and that the ride still opened to the public.

Between 1978 and 1996, at least six people are known to have died. Visitors were known to report that survival was not assured, but if you did, you could wear the badge of being forever changed by the experience. Given the legendary antics, multiple lawsuits piled up, but Gene simply worked the system, refusing to settle until the plaintiff gave up.

By April 1984, after an eleven-month investigation, Gene pleaded guilty to insurance fraud, money laundering, embezzlement, and tax evasion. Still, the park continued to operate, welcoming more than a million guests, despite two deaths that year alone.

Though advertisements portrayed a family-friendly atmosphere, attendance gradually dwindled as its reputation of "Traction Park," "Accident Park," and "Class Action Park" grew. Great American

Recreation declared bankruptcy in 1995, shutting the gates in July 1997.

Gene would eventually purchase the park back. He died in 2012, and his family reopened the attractions—safer this time around, but the ride was short-lived, closing its gates again in May 2016.

CHAPTER 31

That Was an Expensive Bowl of Soup

Okay, my mom wasn't much of a cook. Certainly, that was okay. We seemed to live out of a can or boxed good. For some people, "cooking" is not their strength. From time to time, we did have some scary items land on the plate, and to this day, I am weary of fried food.

We used to keep the deep fryer under the cupboard with a side dish plate precariously balanced on top to keep the "oil" fresh. The plastic lid that came with this early '80s fryer had long ago melted because, stupidly, we put the appliance away hot, and plastic melts. In reality, plastic and oil are not compatible. The manufacturer could have done better.

One day, by route rather than by intention, Mom took the deep fryer from under the cupboard, plugged it in, as usual removed the plate without looking, and walked away. When she heard it sizzle, she grabbed the fries from the freezer and threw them in the hot fat to cook. I know this because I had been doing homework at the kitchen table.

After the allotted time, I cleared up for supper, and the dishes were laid, ready to eat. Fish sticks and chips soon to be laid out. Mom pulled out the basket and tossed the fries onto some newspaper and then proceeded, divvied the contents onto the plates. It was then that she and I shared a scream that brought my dad and brothers running.

While we covered our mouths, horror-struck, they laughed and laughed. A dead fried mouse sat poised on the top of the heap of fries. Our after thought was the mouse had, between the previous and current use, drowned in the oil.

Certainly, if we noticed the mouse prior to "serving" supper, you would expect the same or better from a restaurant. And that is just what this Cracker Barrel restaurant proved.

While we don't really know the exact situation leading up to this incident for Hampton mother Carla Patterson,[34] we do know that, in the end, a bowl of tainted soup cost her a twelve-month jail sentence and $2,500.

On Mothers' Day, 2004, Carla and her two sons, aged twenty-two and twelve, went to lunch at the Newport News, Virginia Cracker Barrel restaurant. Carla ordered vegetable soup. It was apparently when she dipped her spoon for her first sip that she scooped up a full-grown dead mouse in its entirety. By all accounts, Carla began to scream, and many of the patrons fled, fearing their own food tainted.

The incident gained public relations traction, and Cracker Barrel stopped serving vegetable soup at all 539 of its restaurants in the chain.

At the time, Carla, thirty-eight, was also caring for her daughter's mental disabled five-year-old son and didn't have any insurance. This may have been a motivator for the incident and what happened next. When Cracker Barrel officials approached her about

---

[34] https://www.baltimoresun.com/news/bs-xpm-2004-06-03-0406030294-story.html

a settlement, Carla indicated that after she discussed this with her fiancé, they determined $500,000 would be the ask.

A police investigation ensued, resulting in a necropsy performed on the rodent, which proved the mouse not only wasn't cooked, as one would assume it would be found in the vegetable soup, but it also had no liquid in its lungs. In actuality, the little creature had died of a skull fracture before being placed in the bowl.

Investigators concluded that the situation had been planned in advance. Carla had brought the rodent with her to the eatery and placed the mouse in the soup as part of a scheme to extort money from the restaurant—what may have seemed an easy win for a half-million-dollar settlement and a public-relation saving-face arrangement.

On June 1, 2004, Carla and her son Ricky were charged then arrested. Shortly after, in August that same year, the two were charged in another fraud in Williamsburg for check forgery. While the charges against Carla were dropped, Ricky was additionally convicted to nine months in that case.

In facing the charges of the tainted soup, Cracker Barrel ask the jury to consider the cost of its reputation. The fall out for Cracker Barrel included loss of patrons for more than a year at the Newport News location while the investigation and pending trial played out. Additionally, employees testified for their loss of income from tips and having to foreclose on homes.

In what was determined by the courts to be a premeditated extorsion case, Carla ended up trading in restaurant food for prison grub. In April 2005, Carla and Ricky were convinced of one count each of conspiracy to commit extortion for the Cracker Barrel incident. Carla served her term in Hampton Roads Regional Jail, while Ricky was incarcerated at Virginia Peninsula Regional Jail in Williamsburg.

* * *

And the Next Course Is ... Glass

This scam likely did little to enhance the flavor. For almost a decade, from 1997 to 2005, Ronald and Mary Evanos[35] would claim to have ingested glass in their purchased food. Using alias and moving around, they targeted restaurants, hotels, grocery stores, and bars, claiming their injuries in insurance settlements.

For the most part, it seems the businesses always paid up, likely to preserve their reputation. Reports suggest the Massachusetts couple garnered in the area of US$200,000 working the system.

They kept the plan simple and repeated the proven procedure often. After ordering or purchasing food, they would claim glass had been in the food. Although they had never actually been served contaminated food, in some cases, they had actually consumed the glass prior to the event to add credibility to the con.

Using fake identities and Social Security information, they would file for the insurance. After the settlement, they would move to another location and repeat the process again and again.

In the end, the couple was charged with multiple counts of conspiracy, mail fraud, identity fraud, Social Security fraud, and false statement on health care.

---

[35] https://www.inquirer.com/philly/news/nation_world/20070817_Man_admits_to_clear_scam__Eating_glass_in_restaurants.html

CHAPTER 32

Good Heaven's … Watch Your Step …

According to statistics, more than a million people suffer slip-and-falls annually in the United States, with seventeen thousand deaths as a result. In fact, 15 percent of all injuries at work are related to trip-ups. Knowing that these incidents relate to further escalation of other injuries, such as back, hips, bruising, concussions, etc., which may inhibit mobility and a person's ability to earn, businesses will ensure this is a covered situation under their commercial insurance.

By and large, there are two types of slips that are normally caused by slippery surfaces. One is when the heel of the forward foot meets the walking surface without traction to sustain them, resulting in the front foot slipping forward, forcing a backward fall. Or the rear foot slips, applying force to move forward on the sole of the rear foot.

Clearly, Isabel Parker,[36] aged seventy-two at the time, knew ex-

---

[36] https://www.insurancejournal.com/magazines/mag-news-briefs/2004/04/19/41711.htm

actly how to fall, fake an injury enough for medical treatment, then walk away unscathed, but richer for the ordeal. Further, it would be suspected she understood public relations enough to know how businesses didn't want that kind of reputation—injuring seniors—hounding them and cashed on this knowledge of the system over and over.

Some say Isabel was driven by gambling debt. Only she knows her full motivation, but from 1993 to 2000, Isabel was known as the queen of the slip-and-fall. Apparently, the New Jersey grandma orchestrated more than forty-nine slip-and-fall scams throughout department stores, supermarkets, and liquor stores.

In three states—Pennsylvania, Delaware, and New Jersey—Isabel used the same tactic. She would first pretend to fall on the premises, receive aid from another shopper, then file an insurance claim on the property owner's policy.

During her seven-year career, she used forty-seven aliases, eleven addresses, and thirty-three false Social Security Numbers to net more than $500,000 in claim payments. She was finally caught by a curious insurance agent who ran her address in their system and found dozens of similar claims.

Pleading guilty to twenty-nine counts of insurance fraud, six counts of forgery, six counts of theft by deception and other charges, likely because of her age, she received only four years of house arrest.

CHAPTER 33

Fake Robbery—Insurance Grab

Financial security, for some, may appear to be as likely as the glass slipper in a fairy tale. Living paycheck to paycheck becomes the norm for many, leaving nothing left to face a rainy day.

Studies and statistics show that one in four suffer from financial distress in North America. This kind of stress overload sometimes leads to a "no way out" desperation, and the search for easy money ensues. While there are solutions, these same findings illustrate how many don't know where to turn and are unable or unwilling to seek help or even talk about it.

Direct financial issues seldom land people in jail. However, in their despair, some people will embark down a path that does, indeed, lead to the closed cell.

Imagine being a business owner in a tight economy, where others can't afford the luxury items you sell. What do you do when sales are down, expenses are up, and debts are mounting?

In this illustration, it seems the answer appeared on the silver screen first. Taking a page from the screenplay of a heist movie, these partners decided to fake their own robbery to claim the insurance.

Oh, and timing being everything, they picked the most auspicious occasion—New Year's Eve.

In 2008, Atul Shah and Mahayeer[37] were business partners in the diamond district of New York. They owned Real Creations, a jewelry wholesaler, and Dialite, which sold loose diamonds. The expensive gems were insured through Lloyd's of London for US$7 million.

Apparently understanding notifying the authorities of a major theft of jewels would require a substantial and believable story, they set to work. For the burden of proof, closed-circuit cameras, and to add credibility to filing the claim, the partners hired two men, outfitted them with toy weaponry and costumes. Dressed Hasidic Jews, the actors created and went through the motion of the break-in and staged robbery.

Prior to "action," in preparation for the event, the partners poured chemical cleaner onto the security camera and proceeded to empty the safes, leaving behind only the empty boxes and detritus, which would be thrown around as one would assume would happen in a real theft.

Unfortunately, upon closer examination, the camera footage was recovered, including the lead-up, which revealed the scam. This included the partners' preparation of the area, the would-be robbers breaking in at gunpoint, attempting to spray paint the lenses, then forcing Atul to open the safe prior to binding him as one would do a hostage.

According to the filed police report, the thieves made off with millions-of-dollars' worth of jewels. However, the story began to break down as the investigation revealed the pair was six months behind on rent and more than a million dollars in debt.

Despite the 2011 conviction of insurance fraud, attempting grand larceny and falsifying business records, the missing jewels they removed from the safe prior to the attack were never recovered nor were the would-be staged-robbery actors.

---

[37] https://www.jckonline.com/editorial-article/diamond-dealers-convicted-for-staging-7-million-heist/

SPEAKING OF "STAGED,"

Where the Ponzi and Insurance Meet

CHAPTER 34

Considered the Largest Insurance Fraud in US History— Pardoned by Trump

For those of us who hear the term but are not quite sure what a Ponzi scam is, here's the simplified version: It's fraud, pure and simple, that lures investors to pay profits to those who got in ahead of them and so on to retain the illusion that profits are being generated from legitimate commerce. The fiction is retained so long as new investors are always coming on board and older participants do not withdraw their participating money.

In this con, more than thirty-five thousand people had invested their money into the National Heritage Life Insurance Company[38] for decades, expecting their annuity to fund their retirement years. An annuity is insurance as an investment tool, primarily for retirement, to cover the risk of seniors outliving their savings. People invest or purchase an annuity with monthly premiums or lump-sum payments to have a fixed income stream at a given point in time.

---

[38] https://www.businessinsurance.com/article/19970803/ISSUE01/10009059/former-national-heritage-officer-others-charged-in-asset-fraud

Understanding this as a golden opportunity, in 1993–1994, Rabbi Sholam Weiss, husband, father, and grandfather, utilized a series of complex mortgage and stock frauds worth $450 million to cause National Heritage Life Insurance Company to fail.

Although chartered in Delaware, most of the clientele of National Heritage Life Insurance Company primarily resided in Florida.

Sholam was head of a criminal coalition of approximately fifteen other "businessmen," whose intent to defraud the company succeeded in its ultimate collapse. It is said the involvement of multiple attorneys, at least a quarter of those convicted, and one who turned federal informant in the alliance is what enabled the fraud to continue in secret as long as it did and to the ultimate failure of the National Heritage Life.

American federal authorities called this corruption the largest insurance company failure caused by a criminal act in United States history and something you would never expect from a rabbi.

Growing up in Borough Park in New York, the son of Auschwitz Holocaust survivors, Sholam's father owned and operated a fruit store in Brooklyn. At the age of twenty, Sholam purchased Windsor Plumbing Supply in 1974. Profitable for more than a decade, the company started to fail and declared bankruptcy in the late 1980s.

In 1990, Sholam, by this point, a father of five, became a financial consultant. But by 1994, Sholam started to gain the attention of authorities and was indicted, charged, and found guilty of mail fraud. For this fraud, he claimed more than $1 million worth of bathtubs had been damaged in a 1986 warehouse fire. He served eight months in prison.

Around this time, Sholam formed his coalition and had begun the process of taking over National Heritage Life by writing a check for four million to purchase the company. According to reports, what's interesting is that the group did not actually have the money. They utilized a variation of check kiting, which involves a float of nonexistent funds in other bank accounts as a form of credit. Essentially, they would write a check for an amount greater than what is available via the account balance. How they would avoid the insufficient funds NSF would be by issuing a second cheque to disguise the amount to cover the NSF from an equally nonexistent account. This is to allow checks that would normally bounce to clear.

Once in control of National Heritage, the group began to purchase worthless stocks and mortgages in a series of deals that drained the insurer of hundreds of millions of dollars.

After a nine-month trial, the judge imposed what the Department of Justice has suggested is the longest prison sentence given for a "white-collar" crime. Sholam was found guilty of all ninety-three charges then sentenced in absentia to a Pennsylvania penitentiary for 845 years. Charges included racketeering, wire fraud, and money laundering.

Sholam had to be sentenced in absentia because in October 1999, rejecting the government's offer of a plea, he had fled the country during the jury deliberations. Still in control of a significant portion of the stolen money from National Heritage Life Insurance and using false identities, one of which identified him as "Charles Dick," Sholam traveled to Israel, Belgium, Brazil, the United Kingdom, and ultimately, Vienna, Austria, where he was extradited back to the United States in 2002.

On January 19, 2021, just one of the seventy pardons and seventy-three sentence commutations issued on his last full day in office, then president Donald Trump commuted Sholam Weiss's sentence. A White House statement said that Sholam "has already served over eighteen years and paid substantial restitution. He is sixty-six years old and suffers from chronic health conditions."

CHAPTER 35

A Friend ... Indeed

There seemed no ethical boundaries for this father of three, pillar of his church, and financial planner when he decided to scam family, friends, and fellow church members out of their life savings. For more than ten years, Aaron Travis Beaird[39] sold life insurance, annuities, investments for American United Life Insurance Company, all the while skimming the premium for his own use.

To make matters worse for the victims, when the scam broke, he faked his own suicide and flew to Scotland.

Based out of the Seattle suburb of Enumclaw, Washington, from the beginning, Aaron worked under another financial advisor in the firm Team Financial Partners. There, they supposedly specialized in high-premium policies and annuities.

Managing to skim millions, the scam was well thought out and well executed with no discretion among family, church, or friend. All participants were manipulated into investing, purchasing life

---

[39] https://www.wealthprofessional.ca/investments/life-and-health-insurance/far-out-friday-three-of-the-dumbest-life-scams/186148

insurance, or both while Aaron would skim the premiums into his own accounts.

Often he made no investment at all.

Establishing his own postal box, Aaron created false account statements and redirected the insurers correspondence to clients into his mail. He would then modify the information before delivering it to the clients as though it were direct from the carrier.

In one situation, Aaron convinced a long-time friend who was a commercial pilot to prepay $500,000 in premiums on a $2 million whole-life insurance policy. Aaron promised that this would produce a 20 percent growth in the first year and 6.5 percent each year after for the twenty-year life of the policy. Safer than the stock market, Aaron had proclaimed.

In realty, Aaron invested only $200,000 of the man's money and skimmed the remaining to purchase a different policy on his friend, appointing himself as the beneficiary. That was the fall of 2011.

By the summer of 2012, Aaron claimed the commercial pilot had died and tried to claim on the policy.

The noose on this scam began to tighten when the insured received a condolence card from the insurance company that had managed to bypass the redirected mail Aaron had established. When the pilot questioned Aaron, he stated it was a misunderstanding and that he would fix it. This is when the insurer began to investigate.

At the first confrontation and seeing the house of false policies begin to crumble, Aaron disappeared but not before mailing apology letters, confessing fraud to some of his clients. His car was found near a bridge with a suicide note, but no body was recovered. Instead, he had hired a taxi and fled to Scotland. He was quickly located and returned a week later to be arrested.

Beyond the stolen money, which has been estimated at more than $5 million, are the lost trust, earnings, education, potential retirement, and futures for his victims, and there can be no price tag assigned to that.

CHAPTER 36

It Happens Here Too, Wherever Your "Here" Happens to Be

Ponzi schemes aren't just for "other" places or what some would consider financial hot spots like New York, London, or Hong Kong. Between 2007 and 2011, one of the largest financial schemes in Canadian history bilked thousands of unsuspecting people from around the world out of more than $215 million.

The scam, as is typical of these cons, focused on the more vulnerable of society. Perpetrated by New Solutions Financial Corporation,[40] owned by Ronald Ovenden,[41] they focused on the elderly and retired and aimed at wiping out their retirement income into their own pockets. As outlined in the many articles, they would purportedly claim to invest the money for their clients into a short-term vetted credit-worthy company to obtain a realized financial return of between 7 percent and 9 percent annually.

In reality, the money had been stolen from these unsuspecting

---

[40] https://fraudalerts.nu/tag/new-solutions-financial-corp/
[41] https://www.rcmp-grc.gc.ca/en/news/2022/rcmp-uncovers-complex-fraud-scheme-leading-charges-toronto-family

clients in a sophisticated scheme involving a multitude of shell corporate entities and assumed laundered.

To make matters worse, when investor money started to trickle, lacking new investors to fund the old, and the financial planners could no longer convince their victims that the house of cards was real, they filed for bankruptcy protection under the Canadian Companies Creditors Arrangement Act in January 2012.

Marketing companies involved in processing of more than $198 million of the fraudulent proceeds included Proforma Capital Inc. of Alberta and Argyle Funds SPC Inc. out of the Cayman Islands; the owner was an Ontario, Canada resident who is said to have owned fifteen other such companies in Barbados.

Because these marketing companies were listed as primary creditors in the bankruptcy, the real creditors—the victims themselves— were effectively blocked from filing or being represented to retrieve their lost money.

Although many companies continue to be investigated, in the end, the courts and the Ontario Securities Commission allowed the matter to be settled.

CHAPTER 37

The "Risk" Assessment Was Written in the Stars

Perhaps the transition from choosing investments from astrological charts to embezzlement and defrauding insurance companies was a natural transition for Marten R. "Marty" Frankel.[42] This eccentric con man was a discredited stockbroker originally from Toledo, who remade himself with a variety of aliases into the owner of at least eleven insurance companies.

His schemes range from a multitude of shell companies to cover bogus investments to enlisting endorsements from former anchorman Walter Cronkite to the Vatican to make his business appear legitimate. In the end, Marty caused $200 million in losses to the insurance companies he purchased and pleaded guilty to twenty-four federal counts of racketeering, conspiracy, securities, and wire fraud.

Born in 1954, Marty began his career in the 1980s, starting phony investment companies under fake names. By the 1990s, his Ponzi scheme was being established. He utilized new shareholder

---

[42] https://www.youtube.com/watch?v=Ioid9rS2H7s

investment to pay expected returns and create a luxurious lifestyle for himself and companions.

In a creative twist, Martin approached his con by establishing the St. Francis of Assisi Foundation to invest in insurance companies with the stated, though never fulfilled, intention of funding hospitals. To this end, he received a letter from Msgr. Emilio Colagiovanni to falsely claim the foundation received its funding from the Vatican. In this move, Marty managed to destroy insurance companies over five Southern US states.

Though it has never been established where the original investment came from, Marty purported utilized $71 million to set up a trust, which was then used to take gain 83 percent control of a holding company, Franklin American Group, which held interest in various insurance companies. These insurers included the likes of Franklin American Life Insurance Company, International Financial Services Life Insurance Company, among other smaller institutions like Protective Services Life Insurance Company, which sold funeral insurance. In addition to siphoning off the reserves and premium to invest and then purchase other insurance companies, he filtered the money into his own accounts.

He managed to evade the suspicion for most of a decade before Mississippi insurance regulators became skeptical of the religious links. Money laundering questions arose when they tried to trace the $600 million moved from a Vatican-linked foundation in Italy to a Catholic charity in the British Virgin Islands and then to a trust of insurance companies.

Though first arrested in 1999 in Germany for passport fraud, Marty was not sentenced in the United States until 2004, when he received two hundred months prison time. He was released in October 2016.

IS IT JUST THAT EASY?

Health Insurance Fraud

CHAPTER 38

Taking Advantage When There's a "Known" Need

O ver and over, we see the rampant acceleration of fraud in the health care industry. Too many times this is overlooked at someone else's problem. This case raises the question of the impact of insurance on independent business.

US case *Royal Drug Co. v Group Life Health Insurance Company*[43] brings to mind the impact of offering airmiles or other such incentives on a "needs-based" insurance product.

Here's the question: Is it within the scope of an insurance provider's business to "fix" or "regulate" costs within the market to which it provides reimbursement? Further, if this is allowable, just how much influence can or should or does an insurance carrier apply to a competitive open market? And, if they do, is it still a competitive market?

In San Antonio, Texas, eighteen independent pharmacy owners challenged insurer Blue Shield and three large pharmacy chains, including Walgreens, Sommers Drug Stores, and Rieger Medi-Save

---

[43] https://supreme.justia.com/cases/federal/us/440/205/

Pharmacies. In this case, they claimed price-fixing, which made it impossible for them to compete in the marketplace.

Blue Shield, as an insurance company, has been in business in Texas since around 1969. In or around 1974, Blue Shield devised and completed a mass distribution to all licensed pharmacy retailers in the state and offered them the "privilege" of entering into a pharmacy agreement with them. This agreement would mean for any policies Blue Shield sold, if their policyholder chose to purchase their prescriptions at these "preferred" vendor drugstores included under this agreement, they would only be charged the $2 drug deductible as outlined in the policy they purchased. Under the policy, 100 percent of the remaining costs would be covered.

This offered a fairly sweet deal for the consumer and the vendor but left little choice for the consumer and limited competition for retailers.

In this scenario, if a policyholder chose to go outside of any of those participating pharmacies listed in the pharmacy agreement, the insured—the consumer—would have to pay the full cost of the drug plus the $2 deductible. After, the insured could apply for reimbursement of the $2 deductible and the cost of the drug, but they would only be reimbursed 75 percent of the usual and customary charge of the pharmaceutical, less the deductible, losing out on the ability to have 100 percent of the claim covered.

This created an unfair advantage to those on the "preferred" list and didn't necessarily guarantee in the best interest of the patient.

Here's where the claimants made their case: Because the usual and customary charge was established by Blue Shield, the independent pharmacies suggested that this provided an unfair marketplace. The independent pharmacies challenged the court to consider how by setting the reasonable and customary charges, Blue Shield, and by participating, those high-volume retail outlets included as a participating pharmacy agreement, have set the costs at a level below which small independent pharmacies can profitably conduct business. Because of higher costs, customers would boycott their locations in favor of lower costs and 100 percent reimbursement. Therefore, the ability of the independents to compete is effectively destroyed. The independent has to either agree to the price fix, whether the sale is made at the counter, home delivery, or other, or be forced out of business.

The challenge before the court went on to ask for consideration on the impact to the consumer. Instead of having free choice on where to shop, the customer is ultimately penalized by having to pay more for their choice. The difference between 100 percent reimbursement and the 75 percent if they chose outside of the preferred pharmacies.

The independent pharmacy owners requested that the court consider whether it was within the "business of insurance" to influence the costs of the goods and services for which they provide reimbursement under the terms of the policy. The second consideration was whether the activities in question were regulated by state law. And if looking at the first two, did this create the presence, absence of a boycott, coercion, or intimidation? Further, the challenge contended that simply because the actions have taken by the insurance company, that does not deem them to be within the realm of the "business of insurance."

In fact, in *National Securities*, the Supreme Court held that the "business of insurance" included

a. the relationship between insurer and insured
b. the type of policy which could be issued, its reliability, interpretation, and enforcement
c. other activities which relate to their status as reliable insurers

Although the independent pharmacy owners did concede that the removal of the preferred pharmacy agreement may impact policyholders, this was minimal compared to the impact to fair competition and the relationship between the pharmacist and their customers. Simply because an insurance company wants to enhance its status as a reliable insurer by entering and promoting such preferred agreements does not, the brief outlines, constitute the "business of insurance."

The district court held that despite the contractual agreement between the insurer and the participating pharmacies, this did not require Blue Shield to fix prices or to produce other anticompetitive effects in the pharmaceutical industry. The court went on to suggest, as an insurance company, Blue Shield's sole obligation was to ensure that when their policyholders had their prescription filled that Blue Shield "shall be required to pay no more than the drug deductible for each of such covered drugs." It was unnecessary for Blue Shield to agree with pharmacies to fix retail sales prices in the pharmaceutical industry.

Therefore, they found that the Pharmacy Agreement went beyond Blue Shield's obligations as an insurer and places Blue Shield outside the business of insurance and in the business of *providing* products and services. As an insurance company, Blue Shield agreed to provide protection against the *risk* that a policyholder will require pharmaceuticals. To meet that obligation, Blue Shield is not required to guarantee the provision of services on a "cost-plus" basis or any other basis, which might be more economical than the retail purchase of such products. ("Royal Drug Company Inc v. Group Life and Health Ins Co - OpenJurist") That Blue Shield may wish to protect itself and its customers from rising costs in the pharmaceutical industry does not transform the Pharmacy Agreement into the business of insurance.

CHAPTER 39

Quality of Life and the Disney Vacation Club

At one point, there were four ambulance claims made for the same day; truly, one for each member of the family on different parts of the highway, causing one person to ask, "Did the bodies bounce?" Why were they so far apart on the highway?

Tracy Lorraine Pee[44] of Morinville, Alberta, Canada supposedly made more than 257 fraudulent claims in just over five years to her benefit plan with Epcor and her spouse's plan, considering the more than $280,000 "easy money." During the trial, it was suggested that motivation had little to do with the family finances. They weren't poor and seemingly didn't even need the extra cash. Trial judge Donna Groves noted that Tracy told a probation officer that she just wanted to improve their quality of life.

Married, with two children, Tracy didn't call a halt to the behavior even after she was fired from Epcor in 2009 and court ordered to pay restitution. What had apparently started as impulsive, an

---

[44] https://edmontonsun.com/2013/02/04/edmonton-woman-jailed-for-health-insurance-fraud-with-epcor

easy way to generate cash from an unsuspecting benefit plan, had turned into a routine. In fact, even after getting caught initially, she continued to forge her spouse's signature, making fraudulent claims on his employee group benefit plan, opening a secret bank account to hide the extra income, until she eventually landed in jail.

Between her and her spouse's plan, Tracy supposedly made 247 claims for ambulance services alone.

Why this may go unnoticed for a such a length of time would be because in a typical benefit plan, ambulance services do not normally have an assigned maximum per person, per claim, or per lifetime of claim submissions like other parts of a program. It's important to remember ambulance services can be for many reasons, almost all of which are considered emergency-related. In Canada, ambulance expenses can be in province, between provinces, in country, or out of country, depending on the situation and circumstance, from air ambulance to search-and-rescue, transportation to medical facilities, first on site at an accident, to name a few.

The most common practice for an ambulance expense would have the patient billed first for the service. After the services have been rendered, they would then submit the claim to the insurance/benefit provider for reimbursement. What may have been initially a real claim turned into Tracy copying, photoshopping, or modifying existing ambulance invoices, altering the dates and locations, and then submitting these on a regular basis to the benefit plan for reimbursement.

According to the *Edmonton Sun* article of 2013, Judge Donna Groves told the married mother of two that her "planned, deliberate, and rather sophisticated" scam was aggravating because it was "motivated by greed" and continued even after she was caught by her employer.

CHAPTER 40

Busted

Sometimes what happens in Vegas doesn't stay in Vegas, especially when it's a criminal offense.

For two years, between 2008 and 2010 Shanita Flax[45] was a civilian contractor at Nellis Air Force Base where she worked in the cosmetic surgery department at Mike O'Callaghan Federal Hospital. A joint venture of care existed between the hospital, 99th Medical Group, and VA Southern Nevada Healthcare System (VASNHS). Most of the patients were comprised entirely of military personnel, veterans, and their dependents. Shanita's role in this venture was to discuss pricing and prescribed procedures with patients seeking medical treatment in her department.

Accordingly, if a patient were receiving breast augmentation or breast reconstruction surgery as a result of a medical condition or illness, such as breast cancer or an occupational injury, then insurance was available. This coverage availability was delivered through their government-issued insurance via the military for personnel and their

---

[45] https://www.reviewjournal.com/crime/courts/former-nellis-contractor-pleads-guilty-in-breast-implant-scam/

dependents. If, however, that same person was receiving an implant, such as for the breast, for cosmetic purposes, then there would be no reimbursement for the expense as it wouldn't have been considered "medically necessary." Therefore, patients in that situation would have to pay out of pocket.

Shanita invested a work around in this particular scam, involving those who wouldn't otherwise be covered under their medical care. Instead of following protocol, Shanita is said to have intentionally misrepresented the nature of the procedure to the insurers. According to reports, she took advantage of a loophole and would convince the patients to pay her cash, and then she would turn around and complete fake paperwork as though it were a breast cancer treatment. In this way, the whole treatment cost would be covered by the air force base.

As a note of interest, in 2009, when Shanita was committing her scheme, health care fraud in the United States, including bogus Medicare claims and kickbacks for worthless treatments, reached upward of $175 billion.

Although Shanita was charged with eighteen counts of fraud and theft, she pleaded guilty to two counts of felony theft and received a reduced sentence of twelve to thirty months in prison with an additional five years of probation. In addition, the verdict required Shanita to repay the air force $17,400 in fraudulent billing and refund the $10,000 attorney general cost for prosecution.

CHAPTER 41

Weight Loss—Money Gain—
Insurance Duped—FBI Not Happy

From our lifestyle habits of too much indulgence on the patio to Grandma's sweets at Christmas or having that vacation just around the corner and needing to get back the beach bod, the promise of immediate weight loss is big business in the private health care sector. In looking for the quick and easy solution, what would put a mind ease more readily than a doctor-supervised weight loss. For sure, we all know there's a ton of scammers out there, but promising healthy results in a medically safe facility, there's a natural trust for that kind of business.

Except when that promise too is a scam. Like the triple delight of chocolate, caramel, and nugget, this con was designed to defraud patients, Medicaid, and insurance companies equally.

For almost a decade, from 2001 to 2010, the commercials of Dr. Gautam Gupta[46] were a staple in the Chicago area, advertising his many nutrition clinics in Illinois. Famous for enlisting what he

---

[46] https://abcnews.go.com/Business/weight-loss-doctor-gautam-gupta-charged-fraud/story?id=13885714

claimed was medial science for assisting people in their weight-loss efforts, he said his clinics and treatments could put patients on the permanent road to healthy success.

Here's where words and actions differed greatly. While the doctor promoted medically supervised weight loss, he didn't actually employ any medical staff. This didn't stop him from billing as though he did. Claims from his clinics ballooned into hundreds for nonexistent and apparently unnecessary procedures, which earned him more than $25 million in fraudulent insurance claims.

Interestingly enough, those without medical insurance were exempt from requiring ultrasounds on their thyroid glands or electrocardiograms as well as other mysterious tests. For those who did have medical plans, though, the sky in claims was the limit. The clinic would file insurance claims for face-to-face follow-up visits that never took place and charts that were as fictious as the medical science behind the "proven" weight loss.

In what could only be assumed a means of trying to add to their credibility, part of the prescribed program included doling out prescriptions such as phentermine. Phentermine can have substantial side effects, including but not limited to high blood pressure, chest pains, and psychosis. Team members played their role, complete with costumes. Being dressed in scrubs was likely the only thing the staff had in common with actual trained medical nurses. Yet these nonmedical clinic employees pretended to be authoritative as they treated their "patients" weekly, taking and recording blood pressure results, checking their weight, and then increasing or decreasing dosage of what amounted to little more than an appetite suppressant.

This was not the first time Dr. Gupta's medical license had been called into question. In 1999, he apparently failed to properly apprise female patients for procedures required in completing heart-lung examinations. Added to this, in 2009, the good doctor was accused by the US Securities and Exchange Commission of insider trading. He had purchased $1 million in Georgia-Pacific stock prior to it being taken over by Koch Industries.

CHAPTER 42

On the "Make," On the "Take," And Raking in the Profits

Often wonder about the necessity of the trailing bills for cotton swabs, Q-tips, and perhaps even the toilet paper used after a procedure? This is an example of how inflated bills, exaggerated diagnosis, kickbacks, and more have blemished the historical reputation of American medical giant Hospital Corporation of America (HCA), formally known as Columbia HCA.[47] At the time, the question came down to whose wallet was being lined at the expense of patient care or perhaps as a result of required care?

Money walks, talks, wiggles, and continues to cast a long shadow of speculation over the health care practices of HCA. Dating back to the '90s, HCA had been investigated for more than seven years for submitting bloated bills and expenses, overstating the seriousness of patient diagnosis, and illegally structuring business deals with doctors for kickbacks. The rubber met the road in the early 2000s, when two inactive subsidiaries of HCA pleaded guilty in what was

---

[47] https://www.justice.gov/archive/opa/pr/2003/June/03_civ_386.htm

at the time one of the largest health care fraud cases in United States history.

With more than 162 hospitals and 113 surgical centers owned by HCA in many states across America, the government allowed a deal to be structured to avoid HCA being barred from the Medicare program. In weighing outpatient care and the ability to pay for procedures, compared to an admission of fraud, the government found a deal in the middle. Otherwise, admitting to the insurance fraud would have had these facilities removed from utilizing the program for their patients.

In addition, the US government also agreed to pay $745 million of the more than $2 billion HCA agreed to pay in the settlement to resolve a portion of the civil cases that arose as a result. These civil cases arose because of the individual patients who may have had adverse outcomes from the care they received at HCA-affiliated facilities brought about by their actions.

Still, even though HCA was required to enter into an eight-year federal corporate integrity agreement, whistleblowers continued to shed light into sketchy practices preserved regardless of legal action. While HCA may have paid restitution for the falsifying records, free rent, free pharmaceuticals, illegal partnerships, upcoding, and kickbacks, in 2004, one of their Florida hospitals were found to have larger percentage of procedures performed that stood outside "reasonable and expected medical practices." The suspicion surrounded bills to Medicare for price-tagging treatment costs higher than competing hospitals serving similar populations. Then in 2010, another whistleblower disclosed unnecessary, invasive cardiac treatments accounting for around 35 percent of one of the HCA hospital's profits.

HCA continued to avoid penalty or settlement for these cases.

In 2012, HCA was found to again be providing kickbacks in violation of what the United States calls Stark Law. In Chattanooga, the hospital paid a local physician group rent for their office space significantly above the market value in exchange for referrals.

Then at different locations in 2015, in violation of the False Claims Act, HCA settled for their role in administering unnecessary tests and double billing to Medicare for fetal testing.

The saga continues where, in 2017, HCA settled for their role in ambulance fraud from four of their locations. This "swapping" continued, resulting in another settlement for violation of the Anti-Kickback Statute, whereby discounted emergency transportation was provided in exchange for referrals, dovetailing back to the previous allegations from 1996, when they were suspected of paying kickbacks for referrals for diabetic patients.

HCA seems to have a long history of stretching the boundaries of profiting from health care.

CHAPTER 43

There's a Pill for That …
And Sometimes a Kickback
to the Prescriber

Worldwide, the pharmaceutical industry accounts for US$1.27 trillion (2020) in revenue annually; 49 percent of this income is generated in North America. To put this in perspective, in 2001, worldwide revenue amounted to approximately US$390.2 billion.

With this kind of growth and as a result of whistleblowers, regulators began looking into the business practices of some of the pharmaceutical giants because sometimes medications like Plavix, Abilify, and Avapro were only prescribed because of the additional incentives offered to the prescribing doctor by the drug manufacture.

Though never admitting any wrongdoing, Bristol-Meyers Squibb[48] has had a litany of claims over the years from physician kickbacks to insurance fraud, always managing to settled everyone.

In a lawsuit originally initiated by three former employee

---

[48] https://www.sec.gov/news/press/2005-118.htm

whistleblowers who alleged that from 1997 to 2003, Bristol-Meyers Squibb induced physicians to prescribe their medication by aligning gits of concert and sporting tickets, hotel trips, golf, as well as happy hours with the Los Angeles Lakers. In all, there were allegedly fifteen thousand incidents from 1999 to 2005. Regulators joined the suit, suggesting the pharmacy giant defrauded Medicare and Medicaid because through these actions, their drugs made it on the covered insurance lists.

The question arose: Were the drugs prescribed in the patient's best interest or in the best interest of the physician receiving the incentive?

In 2007, Bristol-Meyers Squibb settled with state and federal government to the tune of $515 million and entered into a corporate integrity agreement with the US Department of Health and Human Services.

The company then paid an additional $75 million plus interest to the US government and participating states to resolve False Claims Act allegations. In this, Bristol-Meyers Squibb is said to have underpaid the required Medicaid rebates owned through the Medicaid Drug Rebate Program (MDRP). This program requires drug manufacturers to pay into the program to have their drugs covered through insurance. Because Bristol-Meyers Squibb supposedly, through a series of actions, underreported the average manufacturer's price for multiple drugs, this resulted in Medicaid receiving less than was their due in payments from the pharmacy giant.

* * *

Consumer advocacy groups in the United States say this is a well-known problem that plays a significant role in driving the costs of medicine and insurance premium. Insys Therapeutics were indicted for similar inducements to physicians through education programs for the addictive opioid Subsys. Novartis too settled for $390 million for their doctor-inducing tactics to prescribe their drug.

TAP Pharmaceuticals was charged with paying illegal kickbacks to have their prostate cancer drug dispensed. They would encourage doctors to offer free samples of Lupron and have the users claim their insurance. This resulted in this drug controlling close to 80 percent of the marketplace for treating this disease. Because of their impact on Medicare and Medicaid, TAP paid $559.5 million to settle with the US government, $15.5 million to participating states, $290 million in criminal fines, and an additional $875 million for criminal and civil liabilities.

CHAPTER 44

From the Pill Mills to the Operating Theater, Profits from Insurance

Surviving accidents and illnesses like cancer or living with diseases like diabetes often results in an invisible condition known as chronic pain. Statistics show that an estimated one in four Canadians (2021) and 20.4 percent of Americans live with this condition, which costs up to US$635 billion annually. Unfortunately, in an effort to eliminate the hurt and mental fatigue that accompanies chronic conditions, drug dependency is often the resulting aftermath.

Ultimately, what most patients seemed to have wanted was a bit of relief so they could get back to their lives. But University of Guadalajara, Mexico, pain specialist Dr. Jorge Martinez[49] who operated pain management clinics in Ohio seemed to see a multimillion-dollar profitable business plan.

People who attended his clinic would only be taken on as

[49] https://www.anesthesiallc.com/about-abc/64-communique/past-issues/winter-2010/135-6th-circuit-federal-court-of-appeals-affirms-conviction-of-pain-management-physician-for-overutilization-a-billing-fraud

patients if they had insurance coverage. Many were already addicted to painkillers, but that didn't stop the doctor from demanding that prescriptions would only be written if they agreed to nerve-blocking injections that he would then turn around to bill thousands to insurance daily. Many times he didn't even bother with a physical exam, just administer the shot, then write a prescription for a week's worth of painkillers, like OxyContin, Zoloft, and Valium.

Among Medicaid doctors in Ohio, Jorge ranked 153rd for reimbursement in 1998, receiving approximately $68,000 in reimbursement. Just four years later, he'd transitioned to more than a million in Workers' Comp reimbursement alone. Dr. Martinez did this by averaging forty injections daily with an average claim cost of $1,800. Each patient would receive about sixty-four injections annually as compared to other clinics, which would administer three.

In addition, he dispensed drugs for nonmedical purposes, claimed for treatments never received, and requested his patients contribute to his rising malpractice insurance costs through donations before he would write the weekly script.

By the time of his conviction in 2006, the doctor was known to have submitted more than $60 million in fraudulent claims to Medicare, Medicaid, the Ohio Bureau of Workers' Compensation, as well as private insurance companies. His frivolous disbursement of known opioids to addicts resulted in at least two deaths.

His conviction and subsequent life sentence were the first involving a criminal charge of health care fraud resulting in death.

* * *

Oxycodone (Oxycontin, Percocet), fentanyl (Actiq, Duragesic), morphine (Avinza), methadone, hydrocodone (Lortab), diazepam (Valium), alprazolam (Xanax), and clonazepam (Klonopin) ran freely in prescription form from this unlawful Kanas clinic. In this time, Stephen and Linda Schneider managed to distribute more than $6 million in narcotics and falsify more than $4 million in insurance claims. Their actions were known to contribute to more than sixty-eight deaths. The prosecutor in the case referred to the clinic as a "Burger King for pain pill addicts."

For this and other crimes against vulnerable people who thought they were being cared for, Stephen received a thirty-year sentence, while Linda received thirty-three years.

* * *

Some research suggests that almost 20 percent of health care treatments received was unnecessary. Understanding that desperate people will do almost anything for money, an Orange County, California medical clinic operator Tam Vu Pham[50] paid more than five thousand otherwise healthy people for nearly a year to consent to unnecessary surgeries so he could bill insurance companies more than US$96 million.

The criteria for acceptance to participate in the Unity Outpatient Surgery Center conspiracy required healthy people be employees with Preferred Provider Organization (PPO) insurance coverage, whereby preapproval for surgeries would not be required. Once accepted, the "patients" would fly in from various parts of the United States to consent to one of several surgical options available.

Depending on the person, the "patient" would have sweat gland or sinus surgeries, colonoscopies, endoscopies, gynecological or testicular procedures. For their participation in this conspiracy, they would be paid between $300 and $1,000 or sometimes receive only credits toward inexpensive cosmetic procedures.

In the end, Tam, his spouse, and his aunt were charged with forty-six felony counts of conspiracy, grand theft, insurance fraud, capping, and tax evasion.

---

50 https://www.ocregister.com/2005/12/29/man-admits-guilt-in-medical-fraud/

CHAPTER 45

If You Don't Like the Way Something Is Done ... Do It Yourself

Blood and bribes are the hallmark of this escapade. For New Jersey resident David Nicoll[51] marketing seemed to consist of payoffs, money laundering, and prostitution.

Having knowledge of the health care industry as a trained nurse and former pharmaceutical representative, David likely envisioned a sure thing when he borrowed the money from his father-in-law to purchase a fledgling blood-testing lab. Enlisting the help of his younger brother, the pair set about marketing their services to local doctors.

Like any good marketing plan, to be successful, your ideal client must be able to find you, trust in your services, and send your business. For Biodiagnostic Laboratory Services, that meant doctors would need to have a reason to send their tests to David's lab over the competition, perhaps an incentive to choose Biodiagnostic.

---

[51] https://nypost.com/2018/06/15/brothers-who-ran-100m-health-fraud-scam-sentenced-to-prison/

When David purchased the clinical testing facility in 2005, he began to circulate with physicians to create interest and opportunity, which would be mutually beneficial. In this, he started to offer to pay for rental office space so he could station a phlebotomist on site to draw blood. Though not technically illegal in itself, the amount being paid were said to be thinly disguised bribes, citing one doctor who was paid $50,000 a month to refer his patients.

Things quickly escalated over the next eight years to the point where medical practitioners were being paid off not just in money, but also with private getaways, cars, exclusive concert and sporting event tickets, and prostitutes. According to David in testimony, the lab's largest expense was keeping up with his tab at an exclusive New York strip club. In any one evening, doctors could cost as much as $10,000, which was doled out in exchange for sending the clinic through high-reimbursement blood tests.

Using a series of shell companies, David endeavoured to hide the practice of paying off medical practices for referrals through sham leases, services, and consulting agreements. Once the facility had the referral, according to the insurer, Biodiagnostic typically misrepresented the actual charges or even double-billed when there was an actual test performed.

The return on investment was substantial. During this time, David's clinic bilked Medicare and private insurers to the tune of $150 million in unneeded, unordered, and often unnecessary testing, calling into question the trusting relationship between doctor and patient and the code of "in the best interest."

The multiyear investigation into this conspiracy instigated by Horizon Blue Cross Shield out of New Jersey resulted in more than fifty convictions. At the time, based on the number of participants in collusion, prosecutors said this long-running criminal scam was one of the largest medical frauds ever prosecuted, including thirty-eight physician convictions.

Horizon Blue Cross Shield first became suspicious not only because of the volume of tests, but as well as the price tag attached. The health insurer sought to recover more than $14 million in this massive fraud.

ACCIDENTS DO HAPPEN ...

But Was That an Accident?

CHAPTER 46

How much for a hand? What about a foot? Does the value change whether it is the right or left or both?

I remember an unexpected spring snowstorm in May one year in Alberta. The snow was wet and heavy. It clung to everything it touched and froze like cement in its spot, weighing down and breaking branches and power wires. Driving was treacherous.

Even though it dissipated within days, and we resumed an expectation of good spring weather, the storm left devastation in its wake. While I may have forgotten the actual date, I won't forget the two accidental injuries: one from a line repairman who lost several fingers from an electrical charge and the other from a fellow who dug out his recently put away snowblower and while dislodging something from the blades, sliced off his hand.

Imagine, if you can, intentionally putting your hand to the blade to collect on your insurance policy. This is an example of you cannot take this stuff up. Truly, no one would believe it. Yet, here again, the truth is stranger than fiction.

It seems, with no other prospects, the sacrifice of a limb was a small price to pay.

In the small town of Vernon, Florida, the 1950s was cruel. They saw the last of the steamboats and rail that used to pass through leave. Even the sawmill, which had given many their jobs, closed down.

In reviewing multitude of articles, one is left to wonder if it was a matter of desperate times call for desperate measures. We could guess that perhaps the first claims were legitimate; however, by the mid-'60s, this small town of seven hundred residents led the way of claims through farming accidents, garage mishaps, hunting incidents, and more. In fact, after more than a decade of self-inflicted amputations, those in the "know" in insurance adjustments referred to Vernon, Florida, as "Nub City."[52]

At the height of these claims, people could purchase a temporary loss or accidental insurance for going so much as hunting for the day or on the weekend in the event of a loss caused by a firearm or other such calamity. In the Florida panhandle, this temporary accidental insurance made many millionaires for the multiple policies purchased with payouts in the thousand to tens of thousands of dollars. Over these two decades, this small area was responsible for two-thirds of all accidental loss of limb insurance cases filed in the United States.

Stories from claimants on how they suffered the loss of limb ranged from the outrageous to the completely unbelievable in any circumstances. There was the fellow who maimed his foot while trying to protect his chickens. A man aiming for a hawk took off his own hand. A farmer made the "common" mistake of shooting his foot instead of the squirrel he'd been aiming at, while another lost two limbs in an incident involving his tractor and a loaded rifle.

Perhaps firearms should have been banned …

---

[52] https://allthatsinteresting.com/nub-city-vernon-florida

Escalating premiums made little to no difference to the purchasing power of the payout. It's true, residents bought policies from
several different companies, and in some examples, the victims of
these "accidents" had as many as twenty-eight to thirty-eight different policies. Insurance carriers couldn't seem to fight against the
scheme which, in the end, made the recipients big money, some even
millionaires. These folks would simply invest more in purchasing
insurance than they earned in a year. The windfall, their return on
their investment, made the insurance a sure thing.

Investigators were sent from insurance underwriters time and
again to this tight-lipped community. One detective reported back
on a farmer who ordinarily drove a stick-shift pickup. On the day of
his "mishap," he happened to be in his wife's automatic transmission
car, where he had remembered to bring along a tourniquet. When
he accidentally lost his left foot, he was prepared. A lucky thing
too, so he told the representative, if he'd been in the pickup, he'd
never have been able to drive and certainly would have bled out if
not for tourniquet in his pocket. When the question on how he'd
been so prepared ultimately came up, he responded that there were
snakes in the area, and he needed to be equipped in the event of a
snake bite. In the end, he collected more than $1 million from all
the companies.

Despite insurers taking many of the "Nub Club" members to
court, the lawsuits all failed. Insurers nor their lawyers that represented them could make the charges stick. The problem they faced
time and again was convincing a jury that regular people would do
such a thing as maim themselves for money.

In the end, when escalating costs didn't reduce incidents, to put
a stop to the mutilation, insurers refused to do business within the
panhandle.

| CHAPTER 47 |

The Humerus Was Still Intact, But No One Was Laughing

An accidental death and dismember policy, sometimes referred to as a double indemnity policy, typically works by paying double if there is a death caused by an accident. However, if no death occurs, according to the limb lost or a dismemberment, the policyholder will be paid a sum according to the value assigned to the loss. While there are cases of people deliberately relieving themselves of limbs for payment, most try to get around the system by retaining their parts.

In a case like this, though, if you are planning on retaining the body part yet claiming it to be missing in a fraudulent insurance action, the best plausible action may be to pick something not so visible.

As a repeated claimant, Michael Earl LeDuc,[53] from Escanaba, Michigan, forged his medical records in an attempt to claim on missing body parts. In 2009, he purchased a $500,000 AD&D

---

[53] https://archives.fbi.gov/archives/detroit/press-releases/2011/man-who-faked-amputation-to-get-insurance-payout-sentenced

policy and a year later attempted to file a claim for $251,000, stating he'd lost his left arm below the elbow in a woodchipper.

What typically tips an investigator off to a fraudster is in dismemberment or faked disability claims, the cheat typically retains the necessary limbs. For instance, if they are right-handed, they will lose the left and vice versa. Money is the motivator; therefore, the ability to retain lifestyle is a must.

To add credence to Michael's CUNA claim, he altered actual medical reports from Saint Francis Medical Centre, stating he'd received inpatient care. Of course, the problem was he still had both arms.

In addition to having all limbs, Michael had purportedly filed claims with Standard Insurance for a serious head injury and a number of fraudulent claims with Aflac.

After pleading guilty, he was sentenced to fifty-seven months in federal prison.

CHAPTER 48

Relying on the Kindness
of Strangers

When a scam works once, why not twice? Special education teacher Candice Lambert[54] from Albany, New York, was considered an inspirational instructor. She used this affection to her monetary advantage and developed a sick plea.

Playing the part in this one-woman show, Candice filed a disability claim, shaved her head, and reported that she had terminal cancer. Students, parents, and other teachers rallied.

Successful in her disability claim, Candice retired to New Hampshire to live out the "remaining days" she had left.

Leaving the school district and out of sight of her audience, Candice seemed to relax into her new role. Then former colleagues saw a local New Hampshire newspaper article outlining Candice's fight against an inoperable kidney tumor and how this saddened a completely different school district. Further investigation revealed how she was also collecting disability insurance from that school as well.

---

[54] https://www.claimsjournal.com/news/national/2008/01/22/86616.htm

This is where the authorities stepped in and discovered she was a serial faker. Claiming for multiple illnesses to defraud the system, Candice had racked up more than US$110,000 in health and disability benefit insurance.

CHAPTER 49

Missed the Bus on This One

I t's true, in insurance, we often, too often, use the adage "What would you do if you were hit by a bus?" It's not literal but provides for a good visual on how life strikes out of the blue, and what could be more impactful than being hit by a bus?

It seems more money is available if you watch the bus hit something then jump in on the cash train to follow, unless, of course, you're caught on CCTV.

In November 2008, a taxicab accidentally grazed a bus. By all accounts, this was barely felt by the passengers. However, Ronald Moore[55] witnessed the whole event. Taking this as a sign opportunity was knocking, he ran to catch the ride to file an insurance claim for injuries sustained as a result of the accident.

Perhaps a whiplash claim?

The problem for Ronald was the whole event was caught on security footage, proving he hadn't been on board at the time of the event. Although the bus, itself, sustained no damage, not even

---

55 https://www.inquirer.com/philly/news/breaking/20110407_Guilty__Unharmed_ faker_who_boarded_bus_after_non-crash.html

a scratch, apparently, Ronald claimed he had suffered severe back issues. This, though, may have been sustained from the sprint down the block to board the bus while the driver stepped off for a moment after the mishap.

It was found later that Ronald had nine aliases and other convictions.

More than the bus fare, Ronald was found guilty of fraud and conspiracy and ordered to pay $1,000 in fine and left with two years of probation.

THERE WAS MORE THAN NITROGEN, PHOSPHORUS, AND POTASSIUM IN THAT FERTILIZER MIX

Fraud on the Farm

CHAPTER 50

Ripe for the $160 Million Pickin'

One of the main reasons a farm organization will purchase insurance is the multitude of circumstances that can present themselves as a risk to crop yield. Severe weather can destroy crops or even prevent the planting in some cases. From drought to floods, unexpected snow fall and frost, to be insured sometimes means the difference between the ability to keep going or throwing in the towel.

Natural and unforeseen disasters can sink any good farm operation. Because of this, there have been many programs established to assist when these kinds of unforeseen circumstances threaten an agricultural operation. In the United States, one such program is the United States Federal Crop Insurance Program.[56] This federal program is funded by the Federal Crop Insurance Corporation, specifically developed to help agriculturalists insure against unavoidable losses from weather, insects, and crop disease.

The process of obtaining coverage involves several layers. Although the farmer purchases the policy privately, the premiums

---

[56] https://www.rma.usda.gov/Federal-Crop-Insurance-Corporation

paid are then subsidized by the program as well as certain administration expenses from the insurance company providing the risk
coverage are compensated. The federal program also reinsures a
portion of the risk.

To ascertain risk and proportionate payments to claimants, the
program developed benchmarking for underwriting purposes. By
establishing a base line, the program considers the coverage by how
much a farm should produce under "normal" conditions. When the
operation is not able to produce because of a natural disaster, then
the difference is indemnified by the insurance. Specific guidelines,
like geographical locations, types of crops, etc., explaining how to
measure and document these amounts according to the criteria are
available.

*All this sets the table for just how motivated some people are when
they set about defrauding.*

Seeing an opportunity to manipulate this criteria, Robert and
Viki Warren[57] joined the program in 1997. The Warrens operated
R&V Warren Farms located in the fertile valleys between North
Carolina and Tennessee. Accounts suggest the couple had about
twenty-six properties in total along Mills River in Henderson and
Buncombe County. For roughly fifteen years, the Warrens kept approximately four hundred acres in production. Their primary crop
included tomatoes, among a number of smaller related enterprises
like tobacco and strawberries. From 1997 to 2001, the Warrens' participation in the federal program saw them defraud the US Treasury
and insurance companies out of approximately $160 million.

Through an intricate set up, the Warrens intentionally skewed
the benchmark and production numbers to file claims against their
policies. In this, they created deceptive planting and picking records,
invoices, and manifests. In filing the faked crop reports, they staged
false weather disasters by having employees throw ice cubes and

---

[57] https://www.insurancejournal.com/news/southeast/2005/09/09/59314.htm

mothballs onto tomato fields, which had been beaten down with sticks to simulate hail damage when photographed.

An elaborate set up this size required a conspiracy of participants. In addition to the prosecution of the Warrens in 2003, insurance agents—who profited from the commissions in the tune of $250,000—and the insurance adjuster also entered guilty pleas.

Originally, the Warrens were charged with twenty-two counts of making false statements, five counts of mail fraud, and fifteen counts of money laundering and conspiracy to commit the same. Other accomplices were charged with making false statements, perjury, and obstruction of justice. A plea agreement saw the Warrens pleaded guilty to one count of conspiracy and making false statements.

As the ringleader, Robert Warren was also charged as the organizer, manager, and supervisor of continuing financial crimes. He pleaded guilty to an additional count of conspiracy to commit money laundering, while Viki Warren added to her charges one count of mail fraud for false crop records in a lawsuit the Warrens filed against Patten Seed Co.

In sentencing, the Warrens were required to pay $9,150,603 in restitution as well as $7.3 million forfeiture money, representing the proceeds of the fraud. In an effort to collect on the enforcement, the United States seized properties from defendants.

As a consequence of the magnitude of this fraud, the Department of Agriculture, which oversees the program, has now begun using satellites to spy on farmland.

CHAPTER 51

No Bull Here ...

You may not know this, though it does make sense: One of the oldest forms of currency is cattle. Consider when financial leaders reference the economy with the "bull market" descriptor. The bull's horns swiping upward suggest an upswing in the stock market.

As Shakespeare put so eloquently *In Much Ado about Nothing*,[58]

> *I think he thinks upon the savage bull. Tush, fear not, man; we'll tip thy horns with gold And all Europa shall rejoice at thee, As once Europa did at lusty Jove, When he would play the noble beast in love.*

In fact, references suggest cows were domesticated and then traded up to nine thousand years ago. Columbus brought herds to the New World with him, and Cortez expanded this to Mexico a couple of decades later.

It follows then that throughout the ages, insurance has been

---

[58] https://shakespeare.folger.edu/shakespeares-works/much-ado-about-nothing/

there to cover loss, if any. And just with everything else, as soon as insurance is involved, so too comes the odd misadventure into fraud.

Take Gabriel Parks[59] from Kingsport, Virginia, who claimed that seventeen of his cows had been killed by lightning in 2013 to collect on the insurance. His coconspirator was veterinarian Dr. Bill Fuller, who not only charged for his services but also falsely stated that the hooves had been blown off for Gabriel to file a $20,000 loss claim. The doctor may have mentioned that he also sat on the board of directors for the Virginia Farm Bureau Insurance company.

They may have at least aligned their claim with the weather. Not only were there no reported lightning strikes in the area at the time of the event, but also the cows were still alive—hooves intact.

* * *

In India, to file an insurance claim for livestock, a part of the animal's ear with a tag must be submitted with the claim paperwork. This has resulted in many live animals being maimed.

Cow rustling is still active, adding to the high incident of fraudulent claims in the millions of dollars. In some cases, the industry is looking at facial recognition to tackle the rising problem.

* * *

Exeter cattle broker Justin Tyler Greer[60] was arrested in 2018 on a $1.5 million fraud charge relating back to stolen cattle from California, Colorado, and Wyoming, involving seven victims.

* * *

---

[59] https://www.timesnews.net/news/local-news/kingsport-man-sentenced-for-fraudulent-insurance-claim-on-cattle/article_d2b1aefb-5921-5e2c-80bd-1a9820eb803a.html

[60] https://www.agweek.com/business/arrest-made-in-four-state-cattle-rustling-fraud-embezzlement-case

Or Wichita Falls man Howard Lee Hinkle[61] suggested he had eight thousand phantom cattle on several properties, which he used as collateral in a $5.8 million fraud scheme. It seems First United Bank didn't appreciate not being able to collect on the outstanding balance.

[61] https://www.dallasnews.com/news/crime/2018/06/28/texan-who-put-up-phantom-cattle-as-collateral-jailed-in-5-8-million-fraud-case/

CHAPTER 52

Horse Lovers Beware: Gruesome Equestrian Scandal

Imagine you've tossed a coin to purchase a thoroughbred in antic-ipation of that horse becoming a champion show jumper or racer, only to discover the value paid never pans out.

Horses too are insured against loss of life or accident, which would prevent them from reaching their potential. Although the practice likely existed prior to this massive investigation, between the 1970s and mid-1990s, somewhere in the neighborhood of fifty to one hundred horses in the equestrian world were killed for the insurance payout.

From owners to horse dealers, veterinarians, and everyone in between, the conspiracy was widespread, including, some suggest, Chicago mob involvement. In the end, the FBI indicted thirty-six people for insurance fraud, mail and wire fraud, obstruction of jus-tice, extortion, racketeering, and animal cruelty.

The death of multimillionaire heiress Helen Brach[62] is also

---

[62] https://www.washingtonpost.com/archive/politics/1994/07/28/man-charged-in-disappearance-of-heiress/3ed47704-500b-454f-8bc0-e1494573ef77/

linked to this crime. After her husband Frank Brach's death in 1970, through a relationship with a horse dealer Richard Bailey, she became interested in horses and the sport. Helen even used some of her fortune to set up an animal rights foundation.

Richard's brother Paul sold Helen a number of horses worth significantly less than what she paid. It is suggested that this was part of a racketeering scheme lead by Chicago mob to swindle money from wealthy individuals, primarily elderly women. Before the owners became aware of the overvalued worth of the animal, the horse would be killed in some manner.

Investigations suggest Helen found out that she had been swindled. Apparently, she uncovered information of the widespread scheme, the major fraud, and threatened to go to the authorities. Fearing her as a risk to the continuation of the practice, she was supposedly targeted to be stopped.

Helen was last seen departing the Mayo Clinic in Minnesota on February 17, 1977. She was sixty-five at the time of her disappearance. It is implied that she was kidnapped, beaten, shot, and disposed of in a steel furnace to protect the continued conspiracy of killing horses for the insurance payout.

At the time of her disappearance, Helen was worth more than $20 million. By the time she was declared legally dead, seven years later, that fortune had matured to more than $30 million. The growth of her untouchable fortune continues to this day in the hundreds of millions of dollars via a foundation in her name. Each year this foundation provides grants for animal welfare groups, schools, homeless, and numerous Chicago churches.

CHAPTER 53

The Draw of the Cute Critter Pics

Which lead to insurance fraud.

Let's face it, we all get roped into the furred animal pic in one position or another depicting what we imagine universal love, relationship, or downright skepticism over a certain predicament. The curated tilt of the head. The photoshopped raised brows.

But did you ever think you would claim one of those animals as your own to collect on insurance?

Okay, so let's imagine that you did consider this as a possibility for some easy cash … You know, at the end of a movie that is heavy in animal "characters," there is the disclaimer "No animals were injured or harmed during the filming." Yevgeniy Samsonov[63] from Tacoma, Washington, should have added that to his fictional representations.

True, Yevgeniy had been in a car crash in 2009, to which he filed insurance claims for injuries sustained to him and his person

---

[63] https://www.kiro7.com/news/man-20k-claim-fake-dead-cat-be-sentenced/246645883/

and then the subsequent medical treatments for recovery; however, his pet cat was not involved. Still, that didn't stop him from trying to file a $20,000 death claim for the intense sentimental value of his feline friend that had been "like a son." Or so he wrote within the claim documents. *Cue side-tilting head of your favorite creature.*

When the insurer denied the claim, Yevgeniy went online to photoshop proof of his four-legged pal and sent the pictures to the insurer. It wasn't hard for the insurer to find the exact website where Yevgeniy had snagged the fluffy pics.

Parroting this operation, it seems, in the event that this first attempt didn't pay, Yevgeniy hedged his bets by attempting the same $20,000 scam, albeit with a different insurance company, based on a dead parrot. At this point, we can almost hear the pirate coming out. "Arrr, matey, it's sure to work this time." Except for the fact that he sent in picture of a parakeet as proof of claim.

His third attempt, also not a charm when he tried to file for compensation for lost wages as a result of another accident. Instead, this netted him theft, felony, and insurance fraud charges.

HOME INSURANCE

What's it all worth?

CHAPTER 54

Not Covered and Not Guilty …

It's not hard to imagine raccoons breaking and entering. How many times do people go to their cabin or a farm building and find critters have taken the building on as their new home? Equally, not a far stretch to visualize the aftermath cleanup. But to consider or even go forth with filing charges and an insurance claim? That's a little harder to turn the mind's eye.

In the end, for this particular situation, the question in court came down to, did the racoons—the number was unclear—deliberately and maliciously target the plaintiff's dwelling with the intention to vandalize?

Despite not apprehending the culprits and these furred instigators not having legal representation in court, the raccoon(s) were found not guilty. The ultimate argument determined these terms could not be applied, despite several attempts over the years in many court cases to try to find the four-legged menaces culpable.

Always the conclusion was that these criminal and contract laws were made for the human race, not those of the animal kingdom.

This situation, in particular, was the case of *Capital Flip, LLC v American Modern Select Insurance Company* (W.D. Pa. 1999).[64]

As a bit of background, in April 2018, the masked (the coloring on their fur making them look as though they wear a mask) four-legged bandits entered Capital Flip's dwelling in Pittsburgh. The purchased coverage outlined in their dwelling insurance policy issued by American Modern allowed for a limited number of "perils insured against." When they filed their claim, however, based on the coverage purchased, the only relevant peril in the contract was the "vandalism or malicious mischief." After discovering the substantial destruction, the policyholder made a claim, which was declined via a letter from the insurer on May 6, 2018.

By the end of the year, Capital Flip followed this up by filing a complaint in the Court of Common Pleas of Allegheny County, Pennsylvania, asserting a breach of contract and insurance bad faith had been committed. The insurer, American Modern, countered by contending that raccoons, nor other animals, via several other court decisions over the years, from deer to bobcats, cannot commit such acts or be held responsible for them. In addition to there being no covered liability for this incident, there was also no breach of contract or insurance bad faith.

This is because insurance policies are considered contracts and applicable only to people. The contract interpretation, therefore, requires ordinary principles of contract law.

Through the courts, the legal representation for Capital Flip pushed the question of was the wording in the named peril policy too vague to not consider animal damage as falling under the coverage outlined in "vandalism or malicious mischief" clause?

In this case, lawyers argued, there is only action, not premeditation. In fact, the *Oxford Dictionary* defines a "vandal" as "a *person* who deliberately destroys or damages property." By the same, "malicious" is described as "deliberate acts by a *person* which are intended

---

[64] https://casetext.com/case/capital-flip-llc-v-am-modern-select-ins-co

to do harm." Basically, in both definition of terms, there must be a willful misconduct by a human being.

Based on this, the common usage of the terms would preclude their application to the actions of animals. Specific to this case, the Commonwealth of Pennsylvania declared the actions of these raccoons could not be deemed to have arisen from either "vandalism" or "malicious mischief" because they do not have the moral or conscious agency to formulate the intent needed to engage in such acts or, for that matter, any other criminal or actionable conduct. They are, therefore, not subjects of human law.

By the time this case had run its course, as one insurance lawyer said, had Capital Flip purchased an "all risk" policy, which is, in fact, the norm, then all "risks," including these supposedly intentional animals seeking to destroy their dwelling, would have been covered as a means of "all risks of physical loss or damage." The case law interpreting these kinds of policies is settled and policyholder-friendly. Still, if there is a claim, insurance policy wording is all that matters, especially the limitations and exclusions clauses.

◇ **CHAPTER 55** ◇

Breaking Bad … The Realities

What happens when your tenant decides to make fiction a reality? What's the recourse for the homeowner versus the renter? This is the situation faced by a Nebraska property owner who was left to clean up the pollutants from methamphetamines.

Let's be honest: It's not hard to imagine that this situation can happen to anyone who rents out their property.

For about a year, from April 2012 to May 2013, homeowner Jeremy Kaiser[65] rented his Omaha property to tenants who either used or manufactured methamphetamines. It is not clear which as both inflict significant damage. Based on this case, it didn't matter which action was committed. Jeremy did not regularly inspect the property until February 2013 when a neighbor reported the drug use. Thereafter, in April, one of the residents was arrested and the property vacated in May.

A bio-inspection service found methamphetamine vapors and residue throughout the home and determined that the house needed

---

[65] https://www.claimsjournal.com/news/midwest/2020/10/26/300128.htm

to be decontaminated before it could be safely rented again. Because of loss of income and the cost of significate clean-up, Jeremy filed a claim from his insurer.

Allstate declined the claim, but despite this, Jeremy proceeded to act on the recommendation and spent approximately $38,000 in restoration to make the property suitable. Logically, he would need to do this to make the property suitable for living.

When Jeremy proceeded to file another claim for reimbursement for the clean-up costs and loss of rental income, Allstate again declined, stating the damages sustain were outside the policy coverage.

Jeremy then began legal preparations for breach of contract and bad faith. In his suit, Jeremy suggested that the damages should have been covered as part of the vandalism and malicious mischief portion of the contract. However, the Allstate policy specifically excluded this coverage unless it was incurred suddenly and accidental as a direct physical loss caused by fire resulting from vandalism. Because a meth lab was considered neither sudden nor accidental, the clause did not apply. Added to this, smoke damage from the production of a controlled substance stood outside the policy parameters.

Jeremy went on to argue that the property was contaminated, and therefore, the policy claim should be paid, but again, the Allstate policy contract excluded this causes of loss and that the pollution exclusion applied because of meth contamination at the property.

Holding with the insurer in this case, the Nebraska Supreme Court held that a landlord was not insured for damages caused by tenant's use or manufacture of methamphetamines. Over and over, in similar insurance court cases, two things were confirmed: (1) You get what you pay for, and (2) read the contract, especially the fine print for limitations and exclusions.

⬦ **CHAPTER 56** ⬦

Too Contrived to Be True

Tʀᴜᴇ, sometimes the truth is stranger than fiction. Still, even the truth has to have some basis in what can actually happen, all physical elements considered.

So the question for this fraud came down to was this a series of convenient mishaps or a contrivance for cover-up?

New York resident Nicholas Di Puma⁶⁶ was moving to Texas. He and his nephew were packing and about to enjoy a steak dinner. In preparing the meal, Nicolas had four pans sizzling steaks on the stove in the kitchen and his barbeque grill burning on the porch. Apparently, he was cooking with alcohol, which abruptly caught fire in the pans.

Madly, or so he recalled, Nicholas tried to put the initial flames out with a dishrag. But the cloth also caught fire. Grabbing the pan, he threw it out the front door. There stood his convertible car, top down, and the pan landed solidly in the back seat, spreading the flames. Then apparently, another fire caught on the stove, and

---

⁶⁶ https://www.thedailystar.com/archives/man-pleads-guilty-to-fraud/article_516b29c5-bbf9-596d-b79d-247e6241b790.html

running back to deal with that one, in his attempt to throw that pan out the door as well, he tripped over a packing box. This container then landed on a leather couch, and the fire spread within the dwelling.

No one knows what the nephew was doing to assist at this point. There is no mention of him in these heroic actions.

Still intent to put the flames out, Nicholas ran outside to retrieve two hoses. Why two? One can assume for the two sources of the flames: the inside and the other outside. But alas, there was only the one hose available, so he attempted to put out the fire that had ignited with the pan in the back seat of the car while his home became engulfed by the fire from the sofa. Although the fire department was able to stop the fire, the home was destroyed by smoke and water damage.

Unfortunately, for Nicholas, despite the elaborate details of the well-constructed story, authorities did not buy it. In the end, he pleaded guilty to second- and third-degree attempted insurance fraud for home and auto insurance. He was sentenced to a five-year probation and ordered to pay more than $37,000 in restitution.

CHAPTER 57

Sighting a Masterpiece of Return

There are many stories, perhaps legends, of people seeing a piece of art, loving it so much they purchase it for a song, only to find out later that it's worth millions. Take the painting of Christ believed to be painted by Leonardo da Vinci, which was originally purchased for £45, only to sell for a record of £341 million. What a lottery.

For those who invest in art, they see it as a long-term investment on what may start as a gamble on a particular artist, start buying their pieces with the intent of cashing in on the value of the collection when the artists make it big. Reports suggest art market sales topped $67 billion in 2018. According to a 2019 article from CNBC,[67] looking at auction sales from Sotheby's, Christie's, and Phillips, "Contemporary art has returned an average of 7.5%, and the art market as a whole has averaged 5.3%."

But like all investment, art, in particular, can be fraught with risks, from artists going in and out of "style" to damage, theft, high-tech forgeries, illiquid markets, and we can add to this, insurance fraud.

---

[67] https://www.cnbc.com/2019/12/07/art-has-shown-long-term-returns-that-rival-bonds.html

Knowing all this, consider what the return on an art investment will be, especially when there's no actual loss? For Beverly Hills ophthalmologist Steven Cooperman,[68] that number rang in at $17.5 million then jail time.

The actual appraised values of Pablo Picasso's *Nude Before a Mirror* and Claude Monet's *The Customs Officer's Cabin in Pourville* are unclear, going between $1.75 and $2.5 million in the 1990s. However, it has been suggested that the insured amount of $12.5 million seemed significantly inflated in comparison to even the purchase price. Apparently, Steven managed this small, albeit inflated, feat when in 1991, the paintings were lent to County Museum of Art, where they were left unappraised but insured under the blanket policy of the museum. It is suggested that when he took the pieces back, he retained the insurable amount.

As a known art collector in the 1980s, Steven used his collection of original fine paintings as collateral on a number of loans until the banks required repayment to the tune of $6 million. Apparently, he didn't have that kind of liquidity.

What to do?

In July 1992, while Steven was on vacation, a house worker reported to local police that the paintings had been stolen from his Brentwood home. Although it would take five years for a conviction, even at the time, the authorities found the break-in unusual. There was no evidence of forced entry, the alarm had not been activated, and nothing else had been touched. The investigators concluded whoever stole the paintings would have had to have had a key and inside knowledge of the home and security system.

When Steven filed the insurance claim, the insurers, Lloyd's of London and Nordstern Allgemeine Versicherungs, refused to pay, claiming the inflated valuation did not match the loss. The Monet from 1882 was insured for $5 million, while the Picasso painted in

---

[68] https://www.latimes.com/archives/la-xpm-1999-jul-21-fi-58006-story.html

1932 was insured for $7.5 million. Steven had bought the Picasso at Sotheby's in New York in May 1987 for $957,000.

No stranger to the court system, Steven countered this decline by filing a "bad faith" lawsuit, which was settled, netting Steven the $17.5 million payout.

Steven may have gotten away with the insurance fraud had it not been for his dependence on those who colluded in the crime. It was Pamela Davis, the ex-lover of Steven's attorney, who collected on the $250,000 reward and tipped authorities to the location of the paintings in 1997. Apparently, Steven and his lawyer had conspired to stealing the paintings to collect on the insurance while they actually stored the precious art at a facility in Cleveland, Ohio.

In 1999, Steven was convicted on eighteen federal counts, including conspiracy, wire fraud, and money laundering of insurance fraud and was sentenced to three years in prison.

CHAPTER 58

Fur Does Not Insulate
against Fraud

Investing in the finer things is not confined to art. From expensive sports or antique vehicles, rare and expensive wines, jewelry, watches, vintage clothing, designer fashion pieces, and antiques are also forms of long-term speculation for capital payoffs.

Furs too fall into this category. In recent years, this has been hampered by animal activist groups; still, many retain their coats and garments in insured storage.

This is one those "furry tales" not involving any activist group like Greenpeace. In fact, it seems Samiha Guirguis[69] considered a good way to grab some quick cash was to make a $10,000 insurance claim, stating that the expensive garment was stolen right out of storage. She held the warehouse company responsible for this loss. However, when Samiha suggested that the Philadelphia department store, where she stored the mink in 2005, had lost the garment four

---

[69] https://www.inquirer.com/philly/news/20120622_Mink_lover_accused_of_being_a_weasel.html

years later, she may have remembered that her name was mono-grammed on the inside.

It turns out that not only the homeowner's claim was false. Samiha also inflated the $1,000 valuation tenfold by providing an altered certificate receipt from Macy's. And this wasn't the first attempt. This fur, it seems, had fictious feet. In 2001, she had accused another fur storage facility of substituting a lesser-value coat for her fur.

Caught in her own trap, Samiha was charged with two counts of criminal attempt/theft by deception, one count of forgery, and one count of insurance fraud.

HEY, WHERE'S THE BODY?

Life Insurance Fraud

CHAPTER 59

Motivation: Greed? Love? Family?

I t's hard to contemplate what this family was thinking when they devised this plan. Sure, ultimately, we can assume the money was the motivation, but to go to such lengths?

Clayton and Molly Daniel[70] had planned everything in advance. Yet for all the preparation—the falsified papers, the assumed identity, even the body that would be robbed from the six-month-old grave—perhaps this couple should have read the tombstone. Had they bothered with some risk assessment, they may have realized substituting a woman's elderly body for a full-grown male would be the making of their ultimate downfall.

Or one may assume, perhaps when all is said and done, this young couple from Leander, Texas, was banking on the sympathies of others to rule the result. Obviously, Clay and Molly had rationalized no one would question or look too deeply into the staged accident resulting in death.

In June 2004, twenty-four-year-old Clayton Wayne Daniels,

---

[70] https://forensicfilesnow.com/index.php/2019/01/28/molly-and-clay-daniels-some-body-they-didnt-used-to-know/comment-page-1/

father of two, was scheduled to serve thirty days in jail for the crime of aggravated sexual assault on a child. The offense had been committed when he was sixteen, perpetrated on his then six-year-old cousin. After he served the time, he would have ten years of probation and would be recorded on the Registered Sex Offenders list. As a registered sex offender, Clay would have limitation on where he could live in proximity to school, playgrounds, etc. Perhaps even the contact with his own children may have been limited; at the time, the couple had no way of predicting what the future held in store.

Believing the legal system had somehow targeted her husband, twenty-one-year-old Molly hatched a plan that would allow Clay, an unemployed mechanic, to remain as a stay-at-home dad without any limitations on where they could live. She feared, she testified later, that Clay would never be allowed to see his own children.

At some point prior to this sentencing, supposing this to be part of their overall strategy, the couple purchased a life insurance policy worth $110,000 on Clayton alone, naming Molly as his beneficiary.

With the insurance policy in place, Molly, an office receptionist, began the process of creating a new identity for Clayton. Jacob Alexander Gregg would be Clay's new name. The identity package came complete with a new birth certificate and Texas driver's license to prove this.

With all the necessary paperwork in place, the couple took the next step which included finding a substitute body to cement the masquerade. On June 18, 2004, just days before Clay was scheduled to report to the jail to begin his sentencing, the couple put their plan into action. They chose eighty-one-year-old Charlotte Davis, who died six months previous, to be the substitute cadaver. It is suggested that believing because Davis had been older and a woman with mental retardation, no one would miss the body.

Removing Davis from her final resting place, they dressed the body to look like Clayton, complete with jeans, tennis shoes, and even a baseball cap with a fishhook attached. That gruesome job done, the couple then placed the body in the family's green Chevrolet Cavalier, along with some of Clay's belongings. This, investigators surmised, would make it easier for relatives to identify the remains as Clay. Having scoped out the just right location, the car was steered off the roadside cliff where they set it and the body on fire with the aid of charcoal lighter fluid.

This would prove to be the start of their undoing.

Texas rangers found Molly "surprisingly calm" when she received the news of the crash and her husband's death. This wasn't the only thing that made them suspicious. Added to her demeanor, with no skid marks on the road leading up to the crash site, the police regarded the circumstances with doubt. Further examination proved the fire was started in the front seat versus the engine of the scorched car. Finally, a DNA comparison from the cadaver and Clay's mother proved the body was not that of Clayton Daniels. Then further testing of the burned remains revealed the mismatched gender.

By this point, however, Molly, acting the part of the grieving widow, had coaxed aid from the community and then over the intervening investigation time, proceeded to introduce her two children to her new boyfriend, Jake Gregg. The couple, it seems, were intent on remaining together. In fact, very quickly, the couple simply picked up where they left off. The only changes between Clay and Jacob being that Clay dyed his hair and changed his name. Other than that, the new version remained in the same area and traveled in the same circles of friends and relatives.

Clayton Daniels was sentenced to thirty years for insurance fraud, arson, and desecration of a cemetery.

Molly Daniels received twenty years for insurance fraud and hindering Clayton's apprehension from police pursuit.

Their two children were placed in the custody of Molly's family.

CHAPTER 60

Four Women and a Funeral ...

By the numbers, this one breaks down to four women, three insurance policies, two fake deaths, and a combined insurance payout of $1.2 million.

This California quartet understood the "business" of death. Sixty-seven-year-old Jean Crump[71] was a former mortuary worker, while Lydia Eileen Pearce, thirty-five, owned Steward-Pearce Mortuary in Long Beach. These two apparently came up with a plan to combine their expertise with sixty-one-year-old phlebotomist Faye Shilling and notary Barbara Ann Lynn, sixty-four, to take out insurance policies on two simulated people.

Over a three-year period, the foursome combined their expertise to purchase life insurance on Laura Urich, an Arkansas woman who had actually died years before, and the nonexistent Jim Davis. Though they didn't get as far as the head stone, they did purchase interment plots, bury an empty casket, and even hired actors to pose as mourners for the funeral.

In addition to collecting advance money from the insurers for

---

71 https://archives.fbi.gov/archives/losangeles/press-releases/2010/la080210.htm

funeral expenses, the policy death benefit would be payable to the niece and nephew of these fictionalized deceased. This role of Davis's niece and caretaker was given to Christine Alexander, who was later provided with immunity from prosecution in exchange for her testimony. It would be Alexander who would approach the insurers for the advance on the death claim and try to collect the full payout.

Knowing how to kill people on paper included many falsified records, complete with death certificates. Even the doctor's forged signature was notarized for authenticity. Then came the planning of the funeral, where the caskets were weighted down for the staged funeral. They proceeded to send the inflated bills to the insurance companies for reimbursement on limousine, body refrigeration, casket, and floral arrangements.

Yet so much more than a faked beneficiary and theatrical funeral goes into the claiming process. Used to official forms and administration, as a phlebotomist, Shilling understood this. Phlebotomists draw and prepare blood for medical testing, transfusions, or donation. She knew what the insurers would need on paper to process the claims, while Crump knew what would need to be said when questioned. Shilling provided the location and Lynn the official seal.

The scheme unravelled in 2007, when the FBI became involved after two insurance companies suspected fraud. In the end, it was the doctor, who had previously been arrested in a prescription drug case and been paid $50,000 for his signature, who brought the scheme down when he turned federal informer.

In April 2009, Crump was convicted on seven counts of mail fraud and fraud. Shilling was sentenced to two years in prison after pleading guilty to wire fraud. Pearce too was charged, and Lynn received probation.

CHAPTER 61

Fake FBI Agent Investigated by Actual FBI Agents

Not once, not twice, but over and again, Chicago, Illinois resident Bridgette Buckner[72] claimed to have lost family members to claim the death claims on her employee benefit plan. While employed at Hallmark Services, as a health insurance administrator, Bridget supposedly had a series of misfortunes. First, her grandmother died. Then she was injured in a workplace accident. On April 30, 2008, she claimed her daughter died, and within months, that September, her husband, whom she claimed was an FBI agent, had apparently died in the line of duty. Tragically, according to the file of fictious paperwork, he'd been shot to death on September 18, 2008.

These claims, neatly composed with fabricated medical certificates of death, all paperwork in order, netted her $25,000. But this wasn't her first foray in the fictious killing of family members.

---

[72] https://www.chicagotribune.com/news/breaking/chi-woman-who-claimed-mom-daughter-and-husband-died-gets-10-years-for-insurance-fraud-20110907-story.html

Previously, while employed at HSBC Bank, she collected $60,000 for life insurance claims for two children and her husband.

Unfortunately, for Bridgette, the investigator assigned to look further into these claims was actually a retired FBI agent.

Bridgette pleaded guilty to two counts of insurance fraud and one count of wire fraud and was sentenced to ten years.

CHAPTER 62

The Unintended Consequences of Insurance Fraud

Accdording to the World Bank,[73] China's poverty rate fell from 88 percent in 1981 to 0.7 percent in 2015. By this measure, China's average income has increased dramatically in the last three decades, and using today's standards, most persistent poverty is felt in the more rural areas of the country.

However, for the more than 16.6 million people still living below the national poverty line, desperation can cause people to act without fully considering the consequences. Take the situation of Hunan Province resident surnamed "He." In this family of four, his youngest daughter had epilepsy, and his wife Dai[74] couldn't work as she needed to stay at home with the children. With mounting medical bills, He turned to the one solution he felt would solve their problems. Naming his wife Dai as the sole beneficiary, He purchased

---

[73] https://www.worldbank.org/en/news/press-release/2022/04/01/lifting-800-million-people-out-of-poverty-new-report-looks-at-lessons-from-china-s-experience

[74] https://www.theguardian.com/world/2018/oct/18/china-reflects-after-woman-kills-herself-and-family-when-husband-faked-death

a life insurance policy worth CN¥1 million, or US$144,500, to cover the outstanding credit debt and have enough leftover for his family's protection. Then he proceeded to organize a faked death.

Little did he know that his faked drowning would result in the actual death of his wife and two children.

On September 7, 2018, when thirty-four-year-old He borrowed his employer's car and drove it into the river, it was with the intention of going "missing" for a while. After some time, his family would collect the life insurance proceeds, and then he could return to gather them together and whisk them all off into hiding.

He didn't tell his wife about the insurance policy or his plan.

Little did he know of the extended family pressure his wife suffered as a result of his disappearance. Fully believing He dead, on October 10, Dai felt she had no other choice but to drown their four-year-old son and three-year-old daughter and herself. In a detailed suicide note posted through social media, Dai told of the pressure from her in-laws, who blamed her for their son's disappearance. They apparently criticized her spending habits and scolded her for not working. In addition, they supposedly told others she was mentally ill.

Social media cited that increased pressure removed Dai's will to live. Unable to bear the responsibility of parenting alone and not wanting to leave her children parentless and perhaps a burden on others, she wrote on WeChat, "Without their parents, my son and daughter will be in pain and will be bullied like me."

He surrendered on October 12 and confessed to the insurance fraud.

Authorities confirmed no one filed an insurance claim because He had had neglected to tell his wife he had purchased such a policy.

WHEN IT'S MURDER FOR MONEY,

Insurance Is Typically Involved

CHAPTER 63

Sex, Lies, Money, Insurance

I n 1963, the murder of Carol Swoboda Thompson[75] of St. Paul, Minnesota, made international news. Carol had married her college sweetheart in 1948. By all accounts, she and her husband Tilmer Eugene Thompson had it all: home, children, status, and a future.

Thirty-six at the time of his wife's murder, Tilmer, often called "Cotton" for his white blond hair, was a criminal attorney and the chairman of the criminal law committee of the Minnesota State Bar Association. Obviously competitive and working his way along the legal ladder, Tilmer was said to have had a bright future waiting for him, perhaps politics or even as a judge.

Wife, mother, daughter, friend, Carol, thirty-four, was the only child of a respected local business owner and heiress to a fortune. A housewife and mother to four young children, Carol was active in Edgecumbe Presbyterian Church, Scouts, played bridge, and held coffee parties. In the morning of her death on March 6, she is known to have made a breakfast of bacon and eggs for her husband and

---

[75] https://www.mnopedia.org/event/murder-carol-thompson

children aged six through thirteen, got them off to work and school, respectively, and started her day, typical of any other.

Unbeknownst to her, paid assassin Dick W. C. Anderson was hiding in the basement of their comfortable Highland Park neighborhood home, at 1720 Hillcrest Avenue, waiting for his moment. Then at eight thirty, the phone rang. Carol, who had gone upstairs to bedroom for one reason or another at that exact time that morning, had had to return to the kitchen to answer the call from her husband because the bedroom extension had been removed.

Investigations determined that supposedly on cue, after she hung up with her husband Tilmer, Dick Anderson struck her with a rubber hose. According to his testimony, Dick intended to drown her in her bathtub to make it look like an accidental drowning.

Dick had not counted on Carol's strength. She foiled the plan by recovering from the initial assault. The murderer had been in the process of cleaning up the kitchen when she regained consciousness. Dick then tried to shoot her with a stolen Luger he had brought along as a backup. However, the wrong ammunition had been loaded and the gun misfired. Seeming to panic with this unexpected turn of events, the killer then struck her with the handle of the gun.

Still, Carol fought.

Rattled, Dick then stabbed her multiple times with a paring knife to the point where the blade broke off in her neck. This is the point at which he apparently fled, leaving her for dead.

Like something out of a nightmare, unbelievably, Carol survived this attack too and managed to crawl from her house to her neighbors, begging for help. Help arrived quickly; however, unfortunately, three hours later, she succumbed to her massive injuries of a cracked skull and more than twenty-five stab wounds, some accounts suggest at least fifty, at Ancker Hospital.

As testimony unraveled through the analysis, this may be summed up as a case of what happens despite the best-laid plans. While the police originally suspected a homicidal maniac, the investigators started to build a case against her husband Tilmer, who was known to be a notorious womanizer.

Found pieces of the pistol's grip from the scene led investigators to roofing salesman Dick Anderson, who was an ex-marine, ex-convict, and troubled Korean War combat veteran from Michigan. He immediately confessed to being hired to complete the killing for $2,300 by Norman J. Mastrian, a former Twin Cities prizefighter.

Another interesting element of this story is how the truth was unfolded. It was insurance investigator John Healy who first noted that Tilmer had more insurance—$1.1 million—on his stay-at-home wife Carol, then he had on himself. Once authorities had that bit of information, it was found that just weeks before that fateful March morning, Tilmer had removed the upstairs phone and given the family pet, a noisy dachshund, to a local veterinarian.

Added to this, Tilmer had an almost religious adherence to his daily schedule. On a normal day, he'd arrived at the office at ten thirty during the week, but on the morning of his wife's murder, he arrived just after eight and at eight thirty, instructed his secretary to call his wife and stand as witness that she had answered at home.

Then there was his link to Norman, the prizefighter. In and out of trouble, Norman was a man known to police, and he had been a former client of Tilmer.

Apparently, Tilmer had hired Norman for $3,000 to kill his wife and make it look like an accident so Tilmer could collect on the double indemnity of the multiple insurance policies. Then apparently unbeknownst to Tilmer, Norman "subcontracted" the "hit" to Dick, pocketing the $700 difference for himself.

Further investigation proved Tilmer was well known to have had multiple female liaisons over the course of his marriage, but it was his twenty-seven-year-old former secretary Jackie Olesen, who pushed the idea of marriage to her in particular. This, in turn, it is said, led Tilmer to enact the contract to kill his wife rather than divorce. The insurance money would allow the couple to start over.

In Hennepin County District Court, on December 6, 1963, Tilmer was convicted of murder and sentenced to life in prison. He served nineteen years at Minnesota Correctional Facility—Stillwater. Paroled in 1983, after his release, Tilmer resettled in the Twin Cities, sold real estate, and married Margaret Culver. He died at the age of eighty.

Indicted in May 1963 for first-degree murder, Dick and Norman were each sentenced to life in prison. They too were later paroled.

CHAPTER 64

With Friends Like These

I t's well known that times were tough in the '30s, especially in the United States. The '30s are marked by the era of the Great Depression and Prohibition, rise of the bootlegger, organized crime, and the speakeasy.

By and large, it is widely accepted that "depression," economic misfortune, and general poverty result in greater conception of substances, such as drugs and alcohol. Although Prohibition, 1920–1933, was supposed to reduce crime, solve social problems like prisons and poor houses, while improving health and hygiene, it is widely accepted that this failed. It's true, in the beginning, consumption decreased but then quickly escalated.

This is the story of poor Michael Malloy,[76] an Irish immigrant of about sixty with a drinking problem. He had no known family, and supposedly, his "friends" conspired to plot his death. He was a man with little opportunity and even less of a chance of survival from the conspiracy to murder him and make it look like an accidental result of his lifestyle.

---

[76] https://www.smithsonianmag.com/history/the-man-who-wouldnt-die-89417903/

In July 1932, Francis Pasqua, Daniel Kriesberg, and Tony Marino hatched a plan to kill Malloy, a known drunk who frequented Marino's speakeasy in Bronx, New York. As with the rest of the country, business at the speakeasy was bad. Tony needed the money to keep going, and Michael had racked up quite a liquor tab with no ambition to pay. Of the many customers to Tony's place, Michael wasn't the only one with a tab, but perhaps he seemed the most inebriated and easy to take advantage of.

Michael was an odd-jobs man who preferred to be paid in alcohol. No one knew of any specific trade he may have had previously. No one knew what he did when he lived in Ireland or what his ambitions were when he arrived in America. He simply seemed to stumble through his life in a fog of perpetual intoxication.

According to the reports, it was apparently twenty-four-year-old Francis, an undertaker, who instructed Tony to take out a life insurance policy on Michael. This wouldn't be the first time the pair had organized such a payoff, after all.

Previous to the opportunity presented by Michael, Mabelle Carson had been a homeless woman when twenty-seven-year-old Tony convinced her to take out a $2,000 life insurance policy and name him as beneficiary. As the story goes, on a frigid New York night, Tony plied her with alcohol, got her drunk, stripped off her clothing, then dosed sheets and mattress with ice water. He then proceeded to push the bed beneath an open window and let the temperatures take care of the rest. She died, the medical examiner said, of bronchial pneumonia, and Tony grossed the policy value.

Like the three fates of ancient fables, this trio, which also included Daniel Kriesberg, a twenty-nine-year-old grocer, set their plan in motion. Watching as Michael stumbled in night after night, falling down drunk, and then drinking until he passed out on the floor, they didn't think it would take much to put him over the edge and into a coffin.

Over the next five months, Francis, with an unnamed acquaintance, managed to secure three policies all offering double indemnity. Two of these policies were with Prudential Life Insurance Company and one with Metropolitan Life Insurance company. The policies, worth about $3,576, were purchased under the name Nicholas Mellory, whose occupation was listed as a florist. A bartender at Tony's speakeasy, Joseph Murphy was enlisted as next of kin and beneficiary and would be the one to identify Michael once he died.

As the plan gained form, so too did the conspiracy of participants. The trio had enlisted petty criminals and Tony's regulars: John McNally, Edward "Tin Ear" Smith, "Tough Tony" Bastone, and Joseph Maglione. Gathering at the speakeasy in December 1932, they set their plan in motion with an expected quick return on the invested premium within a short period.

Tony proceeded to stock the shelves with booze and provided Michael an open-ended tab. Michael, though, a hard drinker of spirits all his life, nearly drained the bar dry as Tony's arm supposedly grew tired from refilling Michael's glass with no apparent end in sight. For three days, this continued with no adverse sign from Michael that he was on the verge of alcohol poisoning or death. The conspirators hoped he may choke on his own vomit or at the very least fall down and bust his head.

By day four, someone suggested simply shooting Malloy in the head, but instead, the "Murder Trust," as they came to be known, decided to substitute the liquor with wood alcohol. At the time, it was known that wood alcohol caused blindness but more often death and quickly.

Although they started by tainting Michael's normal whiskey and gin shots with the wood alcohol, swiftly they pivoted to change their tactics and began to serve Michael only wood alcohol shots. At 10¢ a can from a nearby paint shop, the "Trust" felt this was a small price to pay, given the expected windfall. However, to their shock and disappointment, Michael seemed to suffer no ill effect and came back for more.

With the monthly insurance premiums adding up and Michael no closer to the grave, the "trust" decided to poison Michael's food as well. Michael ended up digesting tainted seafood, belched, and asked for more. Continuing to serve the wood alcohol and getting more aggressive on the food, the conspirators let a tin of sardines rot for several days, mixed in shrapnel, glass shards, and served it as though a bountiful buffet. Michael, pleased with the array, supposedly, according to testimony, asked for more.

Next, the "Trust" decided to do to Michael what they had done to Mabelle Carlson. After an evening of drinking wood alcohol until the man passed out, they put Michael in the back of Francis's roadster, took him to Crotona Park, dragged him through the snow, and laid him on a park bench. Then they stripped him and doused him in cold water. The next morning when Tony arrived at the speakeasy, Michael was already there with what he termed a "wee chill."

By February and another insurance premium due, the group decided to run Michael over with a car. To accomplish this, they enlisted the services of yet another conspirator, cab driver Harry Green, for $150 of the insurance money once paid. Holding drunken Michael up, crucifixion style, they braced for impact. The first attempt was thwarted by an interruption. Then Michael apparently managed to sober up enough to leap out of the way of the next two attempts. On the fourth go, Harry apparently gunned the engine to fifty miles per hour and hit Michael, where he crashed against the hood before rolling off and dropping to the ground. Harry, intent on earning his cut, then backed over the body to ensure the job was done.

A passing car scared the group from the scene, and they assumed Michael's death. Days passed with no word from morgues or hospitals, nothing in any of the papers, despite their many attempts to locate the body. Without a body, they couldn't collect the insurance money. Then on the fifth day, Michael, like a homing pigeon, stumbled into the speakeasy appearing only mildly worse for wear than usual and requested his usual.

At the wits' end, on February 21, 1933, the Murder Trust had Michael drink to unconsciousness, where they then placed him in a rented a room on 168 Street, attached a rubber tub from a gas light fixture, and swathed his face in a towel.

Death resulted.

Not wanting to draw suspicion to the murder, the body was quickly buried, and a phony death certificate issued by Dr. Frank Manzella was used to collect the first $800 from Metropolitan Life Insurance Company. However, when Francis tried to collect the other two policies from Prudential, they requested to see the body.

With so many conspirators all lined up for their cut, records indicate that once the investigation started, everyone began talking, and charges followed. The original trio went to the electric chair and died first try.

CHAPTER 65

'Til Death Do Us …

Perhaps this could be chalked up to an unsuccessful version of *Arsenic and Old Lace*, where a bit more patience and timing was required.

Meeting later in life, Columbus, Indiana couple Alan and Tami Duvall[77] had a quick courtship and married just twelve weeks of dating. Within two years, the marriage was breaking down with the pair separated. Added to their personal problems, they were experiencing significant financial debts, including consumer accounts, tuition fees, vehicle loans, and the house was a subject of a foreclosure proceeding.

Some in this situation may question the location of an exit door. Not seeing on, one or the other may devise a means of escape not considered favorable to both parties.

In August 2007, Alan returned to the marital home to repair the air conditioning unit. As the story goes, because it was a hot day, he went outside to cool down, and the couple had a meal. For

---

[77] https://caselaw.findlaw.com/in-court-of-appeals/1614338.html

dessert, Tami had made him a "dirt pudding," and Alan fell asleep and remained outside.

Not bothering to check on Alan further, the next morning Tami returned home from her shift at a nursing home and found Alan dead in a deckchair. She immediately called 911, reporting he likely drunk himself to death. An autopsy revealed that Alan had a blood-alcohol content of 0.436, so her assertion was initially believed to be the cause of death.

The wrinkle, which came out in the investigation, revealed that Tami had convinced Alan to purchase a $100,000 life insurance policy from Motorist Life Insurance just a month prior, naming her as the sole beneficiary. The insurance policy also happened to be purchased from an insurance agent for whom Tami was having an extramarital affair. Upon Alan's death, Tami requested that the body be immediately cremated and proceeded to try to claim on the policy, which was still in its "grace" period.

Suspicious of the timing, the insurance company mounted their investigation, which coincided with the continued scrutiny from police. It was found that the "dirt pudding" had been a poison cocktail, which doused Alan's blood in a morphine concentration of more than eighty times the therapeutic dose of a muscle relaxer.

When questioned, Tami claimed Alan had a drug problem and likely committed suicide. Investigators, though, disregarded this as a probable cause of death since there were no containers or wrappers that would have been present at the site. It is unlikely someone committing suicide would first clean up.

Significant to this as well was the missing medication from Tami's employer and prescription theft from one of Alan's relatives.

In 2010, Tami was found guilty as charged by the State of Indiana for six counts of insurance fraud, three counts of obstruction of justice, and of course, murder. She was sentenced to sixty-one and a half years.

CHAPTER 66

Three May Be a Charm—The Fourth Proved Deadly

Long story short, Elain "Kay" Young[78] killed her husband Melvin "Beau" Griesbauer in 2006 for the insurance money. Like so many crimes associated with insurance, Kay enlisted conspirators to help. Using her friendship, Kay encouraged her friend Katherine "Kathy" Mock to solicit friends and family members to see if any of them would be interested in doing the deed.

As it turns out, the two ended up pulling the trigger themselves and tried to make it look like a suicide.

Well known in her community, Kay was a former superintendent at the Callao School District in North-Central Missouri. In a fourth ceremony, she married Beau, an army national guard, in 2004. They resided on Kay's farm, where she bred dogs.

Dog breeding is how she and Kathy met and became friends.

---

[78] https://www.stltoday.com/news/local/crime-and-courts/woman-charged-in-northern-missouri-murder-for-hire-case-goes-on-trial-in-st-louis/article_8a5020cb-c36b-5bea-b8d3-bbcaa20bf40b.html

Prior to Beau's deployment to Iraq in 2004 and during the course of his year away, Kay purchased several insurance policies on him, listing herself as the primary beneficiary. The total value of these policies amounted to more than US$1.1 million.

Economic trouble was mounting on the farm, and by the time of Beau's death, Kay had circulated that she was afraid of Beau, claiming he had threatened to kill her. Kathy had said she would help her get away and began to ask family members whether they knew anyone who may kill Beau for a fee of $10,000.

In the early hours of March 23, 2006, Beau had died from shots fired from a .30-30 Winchester. The 911 call said that Beau had killed himself, and it wasn't for another two years before first-degree murder charges were laid.

The long investigation found gunshot residue on gloves with Kathy's DNA. A ski mask purchased by Kathy had been found at the scene, linking the women to the crime since they had jointly made the emergency call and were each other's alibi.

Added to this, this wasn't Kay's first kick at the insurance and death for money can; she had previously solicited murder for hire for an ex-husband for exactly the same $10,000 offered for Beau. In fact, at the time of her arrest, she had a new boyfriend, complete with a new insurance policy listing her as beneficiary.

Kay and Kathy were charged and convicted of conspiracy to commit murder for hire and murder for hire, resulting in death. Kay was sentenced to life in federal prison.

CHAPTER 67

The Ultimate Abuse of Trust

There is a church in Baltimore that Pastor Kevin Pushia[79] built in 2005; however, instead of the happily ever after, these are the people who meet at the church, so on and so forth; Kevin instead burned the building to the ground two years later to collect the insurance money.

Kevin worked as a case worker for special needs people in addition to being a foster father of two. Capitalizing on the venerable, in 2009, he purchased multiple life insurance policies on a blind and developmentally handicapped man by the name of Lemuel Wallace. Posing as Lemuel's brother, Kevin named himself as beneficiary.

Using church funds, he then hired two men to retrieve the unsuspecting Lemuel from his group home, take him to the park and into the bathroom, where he was shot to death.

Police began to suspect the preacher who'd obviously forgotten to read the good word, when the insurance company of one of the policies phoned the police as part of a routine check to see if Kevin

---

[79] https://www.reuters.com/article/us-crime-pastor-disabled-idUS-TRE79G7BA20111017

was a suspect. When a search warrant found the pastor's day diary, on the date of Lemuel's death, February 4, Kevin had entered "LW project complete."

During the investigation, it was found that Kevin paid the two men $50,000, out of church funds, for the hit. Further scrutiny revealed that when he and his boyfriend were having relationship troubles, Kevin had also taken out an insurance policy on his boyfriend, in which he was the named beneficiary. Keeping to the same strategy, he'd taken contracts for death hits on his boyfriend's mother and daughter. These were later cancelled when the pair began getting along, Kevin confessed in court.

While he pleaded guilty to conspiracy to commit murder, he was also charged with seven counts of insurance fraud and given a life sentence and an additional forty-five years for the fraud.

CHAPTER 68

Killing a Child for Money

As an infant, Tyrael McFall[80] was born healthy. Just months old, he became the victim of trauma caused by shaking, when his biological father Joseph McFall shook and beat him. As a result, the baby suffered broken bones, permanent brain damage, and was left blind and deaf. For this, Joseph was placed in prison.

Deliberately deceiving the insurance carrier, Tyrael's mother Erica White purchased a $50,000 life insurance policy on the infant, failing to disclose the known ailments, health issues, and impairments. Erica and her partner Michael Schullerman also ensured Tyrael had a Social Security Number, which they used to apply for multiple credit cards. In addition, there were bank and lending accounts opened in the boy's name.

In November 2014, Tyrael, just two years old, succumbed to death via codeine poisoning, also known as Tylenol no. 3, which had been administered through a feeding tube. Court reports suggest that the lethal dose was administered just before eight in the

---

[80] https://disability-memorial.org/tyrael-mcfall

evening, before Erica went out for the evening, leaving Tyrael with a babysitter.

Not long after his death, this Austell, Georgia resident filed for the life insurance. Then while they waited for the payout, the couple went on to apply for and secure five additional credit cards, which they maxed out with purchases and applied for four others. Months after his death, the baby had outstanding balances owing on credit cards he could never have applied for.

As a disabled dependent, the baby was receiving benefit funding from the Social Security Administration. Failing to disclose Tyrael's death to the government agency, Erica continued to pocket the payments.

Erica was charged with sixteen counts, including murder, identity, racketeering, and financial fraud, to name a few. She was sentenced to life in prison plus eighty-three years. Meanwhile, her partner Michael was sentenced to thirty years.

CHAPTER 69

Suicide for the Insurance Payout

O n the surface, this insurance fraud almost reads like a loving dad trying to provide for his remaining son after heartache and misery betook the family. Dig a little further and we discover what some may imagine is a shining example of how opioids ruin lives.

Alex Murdaugh[81] was a husband, father, and prominent third-generation accident injury lawyer in Southern Carolina. His father, grandfather, great-grandfather, as well as other family members were all solicitors for the last eighty years in the region. According to reports, Alex had the name, reputation, wealth, power, and influence. Yet in a matter of a very few years, all this came crumbling down, ending in a screeching halt the night Alex paid Curtis Edward Smith to shoot him on a lonely highway in Hampton County for his son Buster to profit from a $10 million life insurance policy.

As one sworn to uphold the law, Alex, it seems, certainly knew how to break it.

---

[81] https://www.rollingstone.com/culture/culture-news/alex-murdaugh-lawyer-insurance-fraud-1242484/

Investigations into Alex's background have, to date, swirled back to the unexplained 2015 death of nursing student Stephen Smith, who was first thought to be the victim of a shooting and then ruled to have died as a result of a hit-and-run. Then there was the mysterious trip and fall death of the family's fifty-seven-year-old former housekeeper and nanny Gloria Satterfield and how Alex pocketed the death settlement. This was followed by his son Paul's involvement in a 2019 boat crash resulting in death, which he also faced criminal charges. Then closely on the heels of these charges came the unsolved murder shooting death of Paul and Alex's wife Maggie with different guns shortly thereafter.

The spiral continued with Alex's misappropriation of his law firm Peters, Murdaugh, Parker, Eltzroth, & Detrick's funds to finance his opioid addition, which then, some may say, lead to his hiring of Curtis to shoot him so his remaining son would have the insurance payout.

Unfortunately, Curtis, a former client of Alex, in 2013, missed the shot, only grazing Alex's skull, leaving him alive to come up with a bogus story of changing a flat tire and someone driving by and shooting him. Curtis fled the scene and disposed of the gun, which had been provided by Alex. Not reading the fine print of the contract, Alex assumed if he had committed suicide, there would be no insurance payout.

Curtis, for his part in this farce, was charged with assisted suicide, assault, and battery of a high-aggravated nature, pointing, and presenting a firearm, insurance fraud, conspiracy to commit insurance fraud, distribution of methamphetamine, and possession of marijuana.

According to various articles, Alex faces fifty-three charges, including the staged attempted murder, defrauding legal clients, pocketing settlement money, insurance fraud, among others. He remains a person of interest in six related lawsuits and seven investigations. Although police have not charged anyone in the killing of Paul and his wife, they have also not suggested that Alex was involved.

CHAPTER 70

People Targeted for Insurance Then Murder

What do Latiqua Cherry, Shane Paris Sissoko, and Prince McLeod Rams[82] all have in common? They were first insured for high amounts of life insurance then murdered.

Maurice Wigfall was the former boyfriend of Latiqua and father to their daughter. He didn't take the breakup well. Despite the separation in February 2015, Maurice forged her signature to purchase a $50,000 life insurance policy, naming himself as the beneficiary. To cover his tracks, he apparently also purchased policies on himself and his young daughter.

Then in May that same year, knowing their daughter would not be present, he broke into Latique's Maryland apartment and stabbed her several times. Proceeding to remove the fire alarm, he poured gasoline on her lifeless body and set her on fire.

He was sentenced to fifty years without the possibility of parole.

---

[82] https://www.washingtonpost.com/opinions/too-many-children-are-killed-for-insurance-money-heres-how-states-can-stop-it/2017/05/14/f9b4b242-3746-11e7-b4ee-434b6d506b37_story.html

*_*_*

Moussa Sissoko and Tiffany Paris[83] met in 1999, when she was still in high school. Within a year of their relationship, Moussa was in college in Florida and, Tiffany had fallen pregnant. Reports suggest that Moussa had requested that she terminate the pregnancy, but she refused. Instead, Moussa left college and moved in with Tiffany to help raise their child.

At the time of the birth of their son Shane, Moussa was working at a lock and security company and proceeded to purchase a $750,000 life insurance policy on the baby, naming himself as the beneficiary. Despite questions from Tiffany on the phone calls and medicals for their son, Moussa lied to cover his tracks.

On September 15, 2001, just hours after Tiffany left for work, Moussa was alone with the three-month-old, when he made a 911 call, claiming Shane was unresponsive and bleeding from his nose. Although the infant was taken to hospital in Montgomery County, he never regained consciousness, and after ten days on a ventilator, he died.

Authorities claimed the cause of death to be abusive head trauma, caused by either shaking or soft impact trauma. Blood in the child's nose and mouth suggested suffocation. A judgment found the twenty-two-year-old guilty of child abuse and murder.

* * *

Prince Mcleod Rams was only slightly older, at fifteen months, when he was murdered by his father Joaquin Rams in 2012 for the combined $524,000 valuation of three insurance policies.

Although little Prince had a medical history of fever-induced seizures, at the time of his death, in October 2012, this was not felt to be the cause. Instead, the court deemed either drowning or suffocation resulted in the child's untimely death. The insurance payout

---

[83] https://ca.sports.yahoo.com/news/father-found-guilty-killing-3-141028313.html

provided Joaquin with motive in addition to the financial difficulty he was facing at the time.

Unemployed and apparently not having filed a tax return in years, Joaquin's house in Bristow, Virginia, was in foreclosure, so he and his son Shadow were living rent free at a friend's residence. He had maxed his $50,000 line of credit, and Shadow's private school tuition fees were outstanding.

While he claimed the insurance were simply college savings vehicles, the court determined that the cash value was only $984 after twenty years of maturity and hardly an investment for school, the real and true value being only the payout at death.

Suspicious swirl around if this is Joaquin's first attempt at insurance fraud. Considered a suspect in the deaths of his mother and former girlfriend, Joaquin collected more than $162,000 in 2008, when his mother's death was ruled a suicide, but was unable to collect on the policy for his girlfriend's unsolved murder.

* * *

For these and other examples of young vulnerable children and adults, insurance is purchased in secret, naming the murderer as the sole beneficiary. Many policies today can be purchased without a medical exam. Some suggest, in light of the rise of online purchases, that more safeguards need to be in place to scrutinize the amount of insurance being purchased for nefarious ends.

The Coalition to Prevent Insurance Fraud,[84] a pro-regulation group, has suggested in the most recent decade leading up to a 2017 report that approximately 160 cases of murder were motivated by the life insurance payout.

---

[84] https://insurancefraud.org

THE ODDITIES OF FAME AND FORTUNE

Insurance Too Strange to
Be Fiction, You Decide

CHAPTER 71

Up in Smoke

As the story goes, a Charlotte, North Carolina cigar aficionado purchased an expensive pack of twenty-four cigars. Wanting to protect his investment, the lawyer insured them against loss, which included fire. One can assume this was an "all perils" policy.

Over time he had smoked the entire pack and then proceeded to make the claim for the insurance money, suggesting the stogies had succumbed to a series of small fires.

Of course, the claim was declined; however, the man pursued it in court, and because the contract didn't specify the type or size of fire, the company was forced to pay.

Or So the Urban Legend Goes …

But who got the upper hand in this tall tale? The story goes on to say that once the Charlotte man cashed the insurance proceeds check, they had him arrested for arson.

The point is to suggest almost anything can be insured when it has perceived value against loss. Here are some unique examples, most of which are insured through Lloyd's of London:

- Cuthbert Heath,[85] a pioneering nineteenth-century underwriter, supposedly invented unique risk insurance. He proposed insuring a monkey that was a key player in a vaudeville act.
- A Cadbury chocolate confectioner had her taste buds insured for GB£1 million. Hayleigh Curtis was a chocolate scientist, whose taste buds are imperative to her position of sweet innovation.
- Not alone, coffee taster Gennaro Pelliccia's taste buds were insured for $10 million in 2009 by British Costa Coffee. Apparently, Gennaro can distinguish between thousands of different flavors to detect any defects within a product.
- Dutch wine maker Ilja Gort insured his nose for $5.58 million. Although wine making includes the critical necessity of the taste buds, Ilja suggests without his nose, he could not run Chateau la Tulipe de la Garde in the Bordeaux region of France.
- Egon Ronay, a British food critic, insured his taste buds safe for a spicy $400,000.
- Toothpaste company Aquafresh insured America Ferrera's teeth for $10 million during their 2007 campaign.
- No tongue in cheek, KISS singer Gene Simmons insured his tongue for a slick million.
- Australian national cricket player Merv Hughes has his mustache insured for $360,000 between 1985 and 1994. Apparently, these homegrown handlebars were as imperative to his persona as his exceptional physique and superior play. Apparently, forty members of a Derbyshire Whiskers Club insured their beards against fire and theft.
- What is unusual is how, in the 1970s, Tom Jones insured his chest hair for millions.

---

[85] https://www.lloyds.com/cuthbertheath

- Hair care being important, in 1992, Brady White, known as "Santa to the Stars," insured his beard to be ready for his many advertising gigs.
- Holly Madison insured her D-cup assets for $1 million.
- Dolly Parton also insured her ample assets for $4 million.
- Being well endowed, British male stripper Frankie Jakeman insured his penis for $1.6 million.
- In the 1980s, David Lee Roth insured his semen for $1 million.
- And how about those leg policies? Let's start with Betty Grable; 20th Century Fox took out a policy for $1 million on each leg.
- Super model Heidi Klum insured her legs for $2 million; however, the left is worth more than the right because of a scar.
- Tina Turner and Michael Flatley, Lord of the Dance, also insured their moneymaking legs.
- Footballer David Beckham insured his legs for $195 million. However, as a result of his extensive work in advertising and modelling, he also insured his face and "good looks."
- Bending it like Beckham, the Portuguese Real Madrid team took out a policy on Cristiano Ronaldo and insured his legs for $144 million.
- Well-known butt policy was held by Jennifer Lopez for $27 million.
- Bruce Springsteen insured his voice for $3.5 million, while Scottish crooner Rod Stewarts insured his voice for $6 million.
- Keith Richards of the Rolling Stones insured his hands through Lloyd's for $1.6 million.
- This may have been helpful when the IRS came knocking, but it was unfortunately not in force. Abbott and Costello

insured their act against breakup for $250,000. Though they did breakup, they never made a claim.

- For out-of-this-world policies, Taco Bell took out a policy on their Bull's Eye promotion. If a piece of the MIR Space Station hit their Bull's Eye set up on the ocean on re-entry, everyone in America would have gotten a free taco.
- A man by the name of Paul Hucker insures himself for $1.5 million against abduction, impregnation, and consumption by aliens. In fact, there are more than twenty thousand people in America alone who pay a premium for insurance against alien abduction.
- Lloyd's of London is the exclusive insurer for Virgin Galactic, if and when Sir Richard Branson's human space-flight venture ever blasts off. Lloyd's was the first to insure satellites in the 1970s. In a recovering missing in 1984, the insurer financed a space shuttle and crew to reclaim two rogue satellites.
- But not everything is insurable. Stanley Kubrick approached Lloyd's when planning the filming of *2001: A Space Odyssey* against real-life alien invasion before the movie's release. Lloyd's declined the insurance.
- But they did place Cutty Sark's policy in the 1970s for the fictional Loch Ness monster as a publicity stunt.

CHAPTER 72

They Beat It ... In Settlement

While insurance is protection against risk, in some cases, there is protection for "known" risk elements, provided that this is disclosed at the time of purchase. Many contracts will void from nondisclosure when a claim is made for a known risk item that was not divulged at the time of purchase. This was the case when Lloyd's of London[86] declined the *This Is It* promoters' claim of $17.5 million policy on Michael Jackson for his last tour.

Michael Jackson died June 25, 2009, of an overdose.

Lloyd's argued that the policy was invalid because Michael Jackson did not disclose prescription drugs on his application. As Jackson died from an overdose, Lloyd's claimed deception in the case because, apparently, concert promoters had doubts about Michael Jackson's health at the time of application and failed to disclose this and the fact that he had drug-related issues.

In 2011, Lloyd's had filed a suit against Michael Jackson's

---

[86] https://www.tmz.com/2014/01/15/lloyds-of-london-insurance-claim-fraud-michael-jackson-aeg/

concert promoters, Anschutz Entertainment Group (AEG), seeking a declaration that the insurance company did not owe the money. After three years of litigation, the case was settled. AEG said they withdrew their insurance claim because they were reimbursed for losses from the deceased estate.

It could be said that Michael Jackson's death left a hole in the music industry for his talent and genius. Michael Jackson was survived by his three children: Prince, Paris, and Blanket ("Michael Jackson: What's Left Behind - Newsweek").

* * *

Turns out there are loads of artists who write songs about insurance. Who knew? Some notable songs include

- In Chainz's "Waiting for You to Die," the rapper adds music to the consequences of making end-of-life preparations by failing to purchase insurance in the first place, leaving those left behind with the bills.
- In Ella Fitzgerald's "I've Got Five Dollars," the great artist tells listeners of her existing estate plan, including life insurance.
- Etta James's "Somebody to Love" intones the truth of not only about finding someone to love but to also have a sense of humour, good barbeque, and life insurance.
- Jimmy Reed's "Take Out Some Insurance" couldn't be any plainer.
- Drake's "I'm upset" lyrically berates the impact of waiting too long to place a policy.
- Taylor Swift's "No Body, No Crime" gets into the darker side of insurance.
- The Mountain Goat's "Insurance Fraud No. 2" speaks of how insurance fraud is simply a bad idea.

CHAPTER 73

How to Be a Millionaire ...
Or At Least on Television

Deciding to "make it" via a television game show isn't a just show-up prospect. There's a lot of planning and forethought to process. For the popular syndicated *Who Wants to Be a Millionaire*,[87] where you can win your million by correctly answering fourteen multiple-choice questions correctly, the procedure to qualify for that prestigious seat is quite onerous.

First, you should be a fan of the show, understand the rules and how the game is played, and more importantly, your plan to win: Keep up on current affairs, popular culture, and the topics typically chosen as the questions. If you meet the eligibility requirements, then there's the application form. Making it this far is only the beginning.

Almost like a lottery, if your application is picked from the heaps received, typically, you will need to invest to arrive at a set location for the contestant's exam, which needs to be completed within a set timeline. Passing only means you wait to be picked or sent home.

---

[87] https://abc.com/shows/who-wants-to-be-a-millionaire

Next comes the interview with the show's producer to determine if you would be comfortable, interesting, funny—audience ready. You're almost there at this point, and if successful, there's the on-camera interview, and then you wait to hear back if you've been picked, but if you do, here's your shot at stardom and, more importantly, the money.

United Kingdom resident Charles Ingram[88] hit the home run and made it all the way to the hot lights and stage. Most people, though, may not agree that he was necessarily made famous from his appearance and winning on the British television game show *Who Wants to Be a Millionaire* but more for his making it all that way only to cheat to win. Scamming with his wife and a third party, he'd established a set of coded coughs to correctly answer questions.

This was apparently only the beginning. Indicative of what the court termed "habitual" behavior, Charles then went on to be found guilty of insurance fraud.

In 2001, on the brink of bankruptcy because of a £400,000 civil action suit filed by the makers of the game show, the Easterton, Wiltshire, England former army major filed a suspicious burglary claim for £30,000. Additionally, Direct Line Insurance said Charles failed to declare past claims when purchasing insurance and then proceeded to file against the newly purchased policy.

In 2003, the court found Charles guilty of obtaining pecuniary advantage by deception.

A television regular, Charles went on to be featured in radio and podcasts as well as author books.

* * *

Making it this far, through all these examples of insurance fraud, it may be surmised that the first rule in insurance fraud should

---

[88] https://millionaire.fandom.com/wiki/Charles_Ingram

be, if you have filed a disability claim, lay low. It may hurt your case if you are then seen on a reality television show bungee-jumping.

In October 2013, UK resident Noreen Murray, a hotel receptionist, filed a work-related disability claim, stating she had injured her back to the point where she could no longer stand or walk for longer than thirty minutes. Apparently, she had sustained the injury while moving heavy laundry bags. Confusion mounted over the claim when she somehow managed to appear in the *Coach Trip* in Valencia, Spain, within three weeks of the alleged injury. Further, she didn't disclose on the show's application forms that she had previous injuries.

Added to this, an investigation found Noreen failed to report the injury at the time of the incident to her employer. Two days after the injury supposedly took place, she resigned her position when she could not get the time off; she requested to be on the show.

Though she filed the injury claim after and held that she was still injured four months later, the application for the show asked specifically about previous or known injuries. Her answer was a definitive "no," which was then signed and dated within four days of the alleged accident.

So much for it being the "best thing she had ever done" as was supposedly posted on social media. Though the claim would have been worth around £20,000, insurer Aviva declined the claim and filed suit with the Insurance Fraud Enforcement department, to which Noreen was given a ten-month suspended custodial sentence.

* * *

Charles and Noreen weren't the only ones to be enticed by the easy money of insurance and celebrity alike.

In 2007, Garrett Dalton[89] was a Connecticut prison guard on

---

[89] https://www.businessinsurance.com/article/20080330/STORY/100024490?template=printart

a back-injury workers' compensation claim. Seems he was a big Hannah Montana music fan and really wanted tickets to the concert. A local radio station was holding a competition offering the winner tickets. Garrett decided to give it a go and disguised himself as a woman, donning not only the wig and dress but heels as well, to participate in a "egg in a spoon" race.

Being that the event was a radio competition, he likely didn't bank on being photographed and filmed by news crews. Despite being incognito, Garrett was identified, which earned him a suspension, arrest, and of course, a declined claim.

All that and he didn't even win the race.

CHAPTER 74

When the Insurance Scam Arrives in Your Inbox

Like clockwork, the calls, the e-mails, sometimes texts arrive. These have replaced the old-style hard-copy snail mail lottery in the form of an insurance payout from a long-lost relative who has appointed me as their beneficiary. What luck. In a few simple steps, I could come into millions ... if I only comply with a simple verification, like banking, social insurance numbers, etc.

As a group benefit consultant for a couple of decades, I've assisted with a multitude of death claims. From the completion of forms to working with the beneficiary throughout the process, the insurance underwriter will rely upon the consultant to do their part in ensuring the transaction is completed smoothly.

I have had the "never to be expected" experience of tracking down a beneficiary via Facebook. The underwriter had contacted me with the person's name, but they had run into a wall in tracking them down and asked for assistance. I spoke to the employer about the situation, who indicated that the former employee was active on social media. Using the deceased name, I checked his Facebook account. The beneficiary was a connection.

The next part was nerve-wracking, trying to compose a note to the beneficiary that wouldn't sound like a scam and have me blocked. But we had nothing else to go on. Being careful to avoid any "ask," I simply requested a phone call conversation. I included all my verification, the insurance carrier, names, numbers, and how I tracked her down. I think that was the clincher—that I explained the "how" of the procedure.

Amazingly, she responded where I then handed her off to the insurer to take care of the official paperwork.

Then in early 2020, we had another situation where a death occurred with a beneficiary we couldn't find. The adult daughter was listed as the employee's beneficiary, and for some reason, we can surmise an estrangement; the heir didn't want to be found. Almost two years later, the daughter has not responded to any means of connection from the insurer, the employer, or me.

With the proliferation of modern scam artists, these are the exceptions and likely the main reason the second beneficiary has declined all attempts of contact.

Any time a person is contacted in association with an insurance payout, consider seriously the authenticity of this possibility. Also, know that the majority of contacts will be fraud-related. Additionally, insurer don't require your banking information. They can, and more often do cut a check for the payment.

Be vigilant over any telephone, e-mail, regular mail, texts, or contact from "official-sounding" professionals. Remember the "how" of the process and not just the "why" of the communication.

You do not need to provide your personal information, credit card, banking log-in credentials, passwords, social insurance number, passport data to have these conversations. Even when these "officials" provide you with their logo, remember, these can be faked. Verify the "who" over and over.

There is no "urgency" either. This would be money due to you, and it's all on your timeline. Honestly, if you do not recognize the name of the person, they suggest that listed you as the beneficiary, *then clue number one*—it's a phony. There is no such thing as an "open beneficiary status." Long-lost relatives are typically the source of fiction and should remain on the pages of a book.

Question over and again, even when you think it may be authentic on why the person would apply pressure. No insurer is keen to give up money, even when warranted. If they could hold on to the money, my impression—right or wrong—would be that they would prefer to keep it. Look at all the wartime policies never paid. The insurer didn't need to just give this money away.

THE COST OF INSURANCE CRIME

And Those Who See the Signs

CHAPTER 75

The Price We Pay for Insurance Fraud

t is likely safe to assume that if these are stories that make the news, then we have only chipped the barest particle off the tip of the iceberg for insurance fraud globally. Imagine just how many insurance crimes remain undetected.

What's most interesting in being a practicing benefit consultant, then compiling these stories, is people's attitudes toward insurance crime. Like petty theft and purchasing stolen items, participating in the black market economy, this seems to be an almost accepted form of criminal behavior.

The *learning*, if you would allow the term, from these examples is that collusion seems to be an essential element of fraud globally across all lines of insurance. As a crime, insurance fraud has evolved in the last decade alone to include more organized crime. They are cashing in on the opportunity present in people's attitude. With what seems to be relative ease, they convince people that they are "entitled" to make a quick buck or save money on their policies by taking more than they are allowed to claim. There are millions of dollars of profit annually for these practiced crooks.

Then there are the career professionals in a trusted position: health care workers, doctors, administrators, practitioners, those in the legal field, and the retailers who inflate their costs or charge for services not rendered; never mind the average person who sees an opening to take a little more.

In each and every example, there is a good probability that someone confidently thought or said, "Who's going to know?" Based on the statistics, it is more that everyone knows or at least expects the behavior but is unwilling or unable to do anything about it.

A good example of this is the vision care provider offering a "gift card" for people who have vision care on their benefit plan but have no optical needs. Here, we have the collusion first of the health professional and then retail. Because of the "trusted" position, the customer agrees to participate in something that seems too good to be true. Yet they do. Making a choice, this average person attends the clinic, provides their information; the provider files a claim never received for the maximum amount eligible, maybe $200 or $300, then issues a gift card typically for a fraction of the cost, sometimes as much as $100. These folks suggest this is a win-win. The provider makes money off claims never rendered, and the employee receives money in hand that they wouldn't have had otherwise.

Until the rates change at the renewal.

Still, how many times, as a consultant, have I heard "I don't feel sorry for the insurers. They can afford it"?

But can we afford it?

It's actually not that the underwriter can or cannot afford it. The forgotten element is these are for-profit companies, the same as other corporations, and they are providing a risk-mitigation service; therefore, the cost of crime in insurance is passed onto the policyholders.

* * *

The following are some staggering global statistics up to and including 2021.

The International Association of Special Investigation Units[90] suggest that insurance fraud globally stands at 22 percent of claims. This amounts to approximately $38–$83 billion, on average, between 2019 and 2020.

In Canada, insurance fraud costs consumers upward of one billion annually.

In the United Kingdom, for general insurance, in 2019 alone, companies registered more than three hundred frauds a day. This amounted to roughly £11,500 in worth per claim.

The most recent statistics, 2021, suggests that in the United States, insurance fraud costs at least $80 billion annually across all lines of insurance. According to the Federal Bureau of Investigation (FBI), this costs the average household between $400 and $700 a year because of premium increases. In 2021, auto insurers suggested that fraud adds an estimated 15 percent to the premium and costs taxpayers $1.6 billion annually.

With all that we know about the prevalence of fraud, only 1–3 percent of life insurance claims are investigated. Further, stats also suggest that only 10 percent of insurers use algorithms to flag suspicious claims. And authorities typically won't get involved until there is a certain threshold of financial loss to make it worth investigating. Those considered sporadic one-offs are often left off the radar and go unpunished.

While we may at times wonder why the insurance industry, in general, seems to operate at the speed of iceberg with the same maneuverability, this lack of incentive to innovate may be because of this increased risk of fraudulent behavior, especially when online processing is now more than the norm than the exception. About 87.5 percent of polled insurers suggest this is the main reason for limits on products being offered.

---

[90] https://www.iasiu.org

Perhaps the old adage of "We get what we pay for" is truer than ever. We may then combine this with "We pay for what people take."

* * *

While it may seem senseless to point out what appears obvious, with the proclivity for this behavior, this may be the best time to outline what is an insurance crime:

- Exaggerating injuries to collect benefits.
- Purchasing insurance on another without permission.
- Falsifying records.
- Including pre-collision damage in an auto insurance claim.
- Claiming property items *not* stolen or damaged during a break-in.
- Faking a fire, injury, death, collision, break-in, theft, etc.
- Offering or accepting unnecessary treatment.
- Charging an insurance company for treatments that never happened, e.g., through a health care facility.
- Encouraging anyone to participate in fraudulent activity, e.g., through a legal representative.
- Misrepresenting facts on an insurance claim.

CHAPTER 76

The Insurance Investigator

While many times, the insurance community at large relies upon the consumer to spot and report criminal behavior, they also incorporate a number of other resources to combat the rising incident levels of insurance fraud. This may include their own in-house special investigation divisions, hiring outside expert investigators and aligning with authorities to pursue the wrongdoers.

An insurance investigator is not the same as a claim adjudicator, an underwriter, an examiner, or an adjuster. Across all lines of insurance, the investigators are there to evaluate false or inflated claims. Typically, this comes after flag of some sort has been raised in the process. These are the people who can see what others overlook. With an acute focus on detail, they gather the data from all sources, screen the information, question, interview, analyze, work with the underwriter and the authorities to ensure there is no misrepresentation.

A particularly well-known investigator in his time was John Healy.[91] According to pieces written about the sleuth, he was a

---

[91] https://www.nytimes.com/1972/03/12/archives/-nub-city-and-other-stories-of-an-insurance-investigator-insurance-.html

careful researcher able to puzzle pieces together where authorities were focused elsewhere. Whether a murder scene, such as our 1963 "Sex, Lies, Money" case involving Carol Swoboda Thompson or determining suicide versus accident, John would question evidence often a coroner or judge would not consider and determine a different outcome.

By the time of his death, at the age of seventy-four, John, formally of Bronx, New York, was a published author and considered a renowned international insurance investigator. Some may say he was someone to set the standard for all investigations in the insurance industry.

CHAPTER 77

And Yet It Works

Insurance, as a risk mitigator, works every time. As it applies to life insurance, an older now deceased colleague once said, "It's the lottery ticket that always pays off." Of course, being the one sure thing—death and taxes—people *bank* on this every day from both perspectives.

Whether I understood it at the time or not, I seem to have a long-standing fascination with the concept of risk and people's attitude toward the concept. While thousands of people a day will complain about their premium, when a life-changing event occurs, the insurance is usually in the top five steps thereafter: locate the policy, make a phone call, inquire about payment. Make good on the promise of being there when it is needed most.

This is reflected in the art featured in my home. The first one I remember purchasing after university when I had my "own" place, *a loose term at best*, was the 1932 print of *Lunch Atop a Skyscraper*. This photo depicts the workers on the crossbeam of the RCA Building in New York City. Staged or not, it's a marvel how these construction laborers could be so at ease on a slip of building with no safety measures in place. I dare not consider how many, outside this photograph, may have been hurt or injured with no compensation in place.

The second is also a 1930s era photograph. Wallace R. MacAskill's *Morning Dawn* hangs pride of presence in my living room. I saved up and purchased the original. Born and raised in St. Peter's, Cape Breton Island, which is not far from where I grew up, I was fascinated by MacAskill's photographs of the *Bluenose*, not just for their beauty, but by *how* he took the pictures. During a squall or a race, Wallace would tie himself to the mast of a fellow competing sailing ship to capture the *Bluenose* at her finest—racing and winning.

The risk for the ultimate reward, and so his picture of the beautiful schooner went on to grace the Canadian dime and remains there to this day.

The last, found a couple of years ago and a fitting depiction for the cover of They'll Never Know, *is the 1895 Granville-Paris Express rail engine 120-721 crash.*

Behind this Roger Viollet photograph is the story of a series of unanticipated events. The conductor is running behind. To make up time, he retains the high speed when he knows he should be slowing on the approach to the station. Then the Westinghouse air brake fails to engage.

Two other employees could have slowed the train using hand brakes, but they were preoccupied and didn't seem to notice how fast the locomotive was approaching. The lack of brakes caused the train to crush the buffer stop, crash through the concourse at top speed, smash through a two-foot-thick brick wall, and fly through the air to plummet two stories to the ground.

Examining the photograph and the depicted damage, it may seem like a miracle that only five passengers were injured and none killed. There was, however, one person who did die. The victim was the wife of a newsstand vendor outside the building on the street below, who was struck by the sudden shattering then falling masonry.

A fitting metaphor, in my opinion, to the many stories represented in this book.

Thank you for taking the time to read this compilation of stories.

ABOUT THE AUTHOR

Lori Power is an independent group benefit consultant, specializing in designing strategic employee group benefit plans to align with the corporate, compensation, culture, and wellness policies of each organization she serves. Their diverse needs, combined with engaging with employees from all walks of life, backgrounds, cultures, provide inspiration on the moments and stories which are the tapestry of life. This ability to help and engage is the "why" she does what she does and how this book came into being. Lori Power is the author of several fiction and non-fiction books, a public presenter, educator, creator, zoom caster, blogger and so much more.